START YOUR OWN
FREIGHT BROKERAGE BUSINESS

Additional titles in **Entrepreneur's Startup Series**

Start Your Own

Entrepreneur MAGAZINE'S

STARTUP

START YOUR OWN

FREIGHT BROKERAGE BUSINESS

Fifth Edition

YOUR STEP-BY-STEP GUIDE TO SUCCESS

The Staff of Entrepreneur Media, Inc. & Jason R. Rich

Entrepreneur
PRESS®

Entrepreneur Press, Publisher
Cover Design: Andrew Welyczko
Production and Composition: Eliot House Productions

This publication is designed to provide accurate and authoritative information in regard to the subject matter covered. It is sold with the understanding that the publisher is not engaged in rendering legal, accounting or other professional services. If legal advice or other expert assistance is required, the services of a competent professional person should be sought.

Library of Congress Cataloging-in-Publication Data
Names: Rich, Jason, author. | Lynn, Jacquelyn. Start your own freight brokerage business.
Title: Start your own freight brokerage business: your step-by-step guide to success / by The Staff of Entrepreneur Media, Inc. and Jason R. Rich.
Other titles: Entrepreneur (Santa Monica, Calif.)
Description: 5th edition. | Irvine, California : Entrepreneur Media, Inc., [2017] | Earlier editions authored by Jacquelyn Lynn. | Includes index.
Identifiers: LCCN 2017007322| ISBN 978-1-59918-605-4 (alk. paper) | ISBN 1-59918-605-5 (alk. paper)
Subjects: LCSH: Freight and freightage. | New business enterprises.
Classification: LCC HE199.A2 L96 2017 | DDC 388/.0440681—dc23
LC record available at https://lccn.loc.gov/2017007322
Printed in the United States of America

21 20 19 18 17   10 9 8 7 6 5 4 3 2 1

Contents

Chapter 6
Staffing Your Company 79

Chapter 7
Marketing 91

Chapter 8
Sales 99

Chapter 9
Financial Management 107

Chapter 10
Tales from the Trenches 117

Appendix
Freight Broker Resources 125

Glossary 131

Index 139

Preface

Do you understand the concept of being a middleman in business? Two companies or parties need to work together, but it takes a third, independent party to bring everyone together, to make the introductions, and then ensure the business transactions that need to happen transpire smoothly.

The role of a broker is to bring two separate parties together. In a social setting, a broker might serve as a matchmaker and introduce a single man to a single woman. When it comes to buying and selling real estate, for example, it's a real estate broker who brings buyers and sellers together. A stockbroker, for example, brings investors and companies that are selling stock together.

Meanwhile, it's the job of a freight broker to bring shippers and carriers together. This may seem like a simple and straight forward endeavor, but there's a lot of problem solving and logistical work that goes into becoming a successful freight broker.

Of course, when your great aunt Agnes wants to introduce you to that "perfect" person, the only reward she's hoping for is the satisfaction of being the catalyst behind a successful relationship—and perhaps some recognition at the wedding. But in business, brokers expect to be compensated for their matchmaking efforts, and justifiably so. Brokers perform an extremely valuable service, bringing together buyers and sellers who might not otherwise be able to find each other. Brokers assist in negotiating the terms of the transaction, and then often oversee the transaction from start to finish.

Brokers in passenger transportation are typically known as travel agents. Their function is to identify and arrange the most appropriate travel methods for their clients, whether it's booking a single, one-way seat on an airplane, or putting together an elaborate tour package that includes surface and air passage, hotels, meals, and recreation.

On the freight side of the transportation industry, the primary role of a broker is to help companies that need to ship cargo find a trucking company that can deliver the shipment on time and in good condition, plus provide any extra services that may be required—all at a competitive price.

As you'll discover, becoming a successful freight broker will require you to seek out shippers and carriers, manage these relationships, continuously overcome challenges that arise, and work under tight deadlines. Your ability to multitask, as well as tap into your communication, time management, problem solving, and organizational skills will all come into play every day.

Why can't shippers simply find and hire their own carriers in order to transport their cargo? The simple answer is because it isn't practical or realistic for them to become intimately familiar with the service and rate structures of hundreds of different motor freight companies.

Even if they build in the cost of the broker's commission—which the carrier, not the shipper, often pays—most shippers save time and money, plus receive better service by using a freight broker rather than shopping around for freight services on their own.

From the carrier's perspective, the broker brings in business that the carrier might not have been able to find on its own. Unlike an in-house salesperson, the broker is only paid when the carrier hauls a load. In today's business world, carriers have come to respect, appreciate, and heavily rely on the role brokers play in keeping the transportation industry moving. What this potentially means for you is opportunity!

Of course, for freight brokers, there's much more to the process than making an introduction and then quickly collecting a commission. Brokers work hard in a fast-paced, demanding environment. They thrive on stress, enjoy challenges, and have strong social skills (e.g., the ability to communicate with other people in person, by phone, in writing, and via email). If your ideal business includes a predictable routine and a limited amount of human contact, stop reading the book right now, because operating a freight brokerage business or working as an agent for an established freight broker, isn't for you.

However, if you want minute-by-minute change, unexpected crises, and daily opportunities to stretch your creativity and problem-solving abilities to the maximum, you'll probably make a great freight broker or agent.

This book will take you through the process of starting a freight brokerage business (or becoming an agent), beginning with a general overview of the freight industry and the role brokers play. It will explain basic requirements and start-up costs. You'll learn about day-to-day operations when things are going well—and when they're going wrong. You'll also discover strategies for finding, hiring, and retaining good employees—as well as what to do when you lose them. You'll gain a solid understanding of the sales and marketing process, as well as how to track and manage the financial side of your business. Throughout the book, you'll hear from freight brokers and industry experts who have built successful companies and who are eager to share what they've learned from their own first-hand, real-world experience.

By turning the page, you're about to take the next step of your journey into learning more about one of the most fundamentally necessary businesses in today's business world—the freight brokerage.

tip

Someone who owns and operates a freight brokerage business is considered a freight broker. Someone who has the training to be a freight broker but opts to work as an independent contractor for a freight brokerage business is called an agent.

A freight broker must handle the day-to-day responsibilities of being a freight broker, and take on the management, licensing, insurance (bond), and financial responsibilities of operating their own business. An agent has the same job-related responsibilities, without the management, licensing, and financial responsibilities of owning the business.

Introduction to the Freight Brokerage Business

The transportation industry in general, and the trucking industry specifically, are critical to the economic and social survival of local communities, the country, and, indeed, the entire world. Think about the times major transportation systems have failed because of mechanical problems, natural disasters, or labor conflicts.

When cargo can't move, the repercussions are serious and widespread. For example, store shelves are emptied, perishable goods spoil, factories are shut down, workers become idled, and the economic repercussions quickly become catastrophic.

The United States may be shifting from a manufacturing to an information-based economy, and technology is certainly impacting every business, but there will never be a time when goods do not have to move. Thus, the freight transportation needs of manufacturers, distributors, wholesalers, retailers, online merchants, and many other types of businesses is growing rapidly within the United States. Furthermore, the need for shippers to transport their cargo in a timely, efficient, and cost-effective manner can mean the difference between profitability and significant financial loss. This presents a tremendous and potentially lucrative opportunity for knowledgeable and skilled freight brokers.

"Logistics professionals in the United States—shippers, intermediaries, and carriers—have transformed the way we do business," says Robert A. Voltmann, president and CEO of the Transportation Intermediaries Association (TIA) in Alexandria, Virginia (www.tianet.org). "In the process, our national economy has been transformed as well. Transportation has become a strategic asset. Inventory is now stored in motion, as we have

▶ Terminology Explained

Broker means a person who, for compensation, arranges or offers to arrange the transportation of property by an authorized motor carrier. Motor carriers, or persons who are employees or bona fide agents of carriers, are not brokers within the meaning of this section when they arrange or offer to arrange the transportation of shipments which they are authorized to transport and which they have accepted and legally bound themselves to transport.

Brokerage or *brokerage service* is the arranging of transportation or the physical movement of a motor vehicle or of property. It can be performed on behalf of a motor carrier, consignor, or consignee. Non-brokerage service is all other service performed by a broker on behalf of a motor carrier, consignor, or consignee.

been able to move to just-in-time delivery. More goods are being moved with more efficiency and reliability than ever before."

Take a look around your home or office. It's highly unlikely that you have much—if anything at all—that didn't reach you either entirely or partially by truck. The size and scope of the motor freight industry can be overwhelming. This is not something most people think about on a day-to-day basis, as long as what's needed shows up at their door (or at their local store) when it's expected.

The good news for you is that there's plenty of room for you to start and grow a profitable business serving the transportation industry as a freight broker. What exactly is a freight broker? Very simply, it is an individual or a company that brings together a shipper that needs to transport goods with an authorized motor carrier that wants to provide the service. The legal definitions of *broker* and *brokerage service* are found in the Code of Federal Regulations, 49CFR371.3:

A freight broker falls into the category of transportation intermediary, which is a company that is neither a shipper nor an asset-owning carrier, but plays a role in the movement of cargo. "Transportation intermediaries leverage their knowledge, investment in technology, and people resources to help both the shipper and carrier succeed," explained Voltmann.

Brokers provide an important and valuable service, which in many cases has become indispensable within recent years, to both motor carriers and shippers. Brokers help carriers fill their trucks and earn a commission for their efforts. They help shippers find reliable motor carriers that the shippers might not have otherwise known about. In fact, some companies use brokers as their traffic department, allowing the broker to coordinate all of their shipping needs.

Brokers are not new to the trucking industry; they've been around since the industry itself began in the early part of the 20th century. Prior to the 1970s, however, regulations

fun fact

According to U.S. Freight Brokers, "70 percent of all manufactured and retail goods transported within the United States on an annual basis are via truck." However, research conducted and published within *Logistics Today* in March 2016, suggests that during the past decade, larger freight brokers have done significantly better than small, independent brokers because these larger organizations are able to better leverage technology, hire larger and more experienced teams of salespeople, keep prices low, plus use their size, financial stability, and experience as a selling point with potential customers and clients.

governing brokers were so restrictive that few firms were willing to even try to gain entry into the industry. But with dramatic changes in federal transportation policy during the 1970s, regulatory restrictions have been eased, creating new entrepreneurial opportunities in the third-party logistics arena.

The Players

An industry so huge and diverse requires a wide range of participants to thrive. Some of these participants' titles may be a bit confusing, and some of their responsibilities may overlap. But to keep things clear, and as simple as possible, let's look at who the key players are and what they typically do.

▶ *Freight broker.* A freight broker is the middleman who connects shippers and carriers. Freight brokers are also known as "truck brokers," "transportation brokers," and "property brokers." Though the term "freight broker" is used throughout this book, you may see or hear these other titles elsewhere.

▶ *Shipper.* A shipper is an entity that has products or goods to transport. Technically, shippers can be individuals or companies, but as a broker, you will deal most often with businesses in fields like manufacturing or agriculture.

▶ *Motor carrier.* A motor carrier is a company that provides truck transportation. There are two types of motor carriers: private (a company that provides truck transportation of its own cargo), and for hire (a company that is paid to provide truck transportation of cargo belonging to others). There are two types of for-hire carriers: common and contract. A common carrier serves the public under two stringent obligations: compulsory service and liability for loss or damage to goods. A contract carrier transports freight under contract with one or a limited number of shippers.

▶ *Freight forwarder.* Often confused with freight brokers, freight forwarders are significantly different. Forwarders typically take possession of the goods, consolidate numerous smaller shipments into one large shipment, then arrange for

tip

Many shippers who have their own fleets (private carriers) occasionally function as contract carriers. Many of their trips are one way, and they often work with brokers to find loads to carry on their return trips. Build relationships with private carriers whenever you can.

transport of that larger shipment. To transport goods, surface freight forwarders use both motor freight and rail carriage; airfreight forwarders use cargo and passenger airlines; and ocean freight forwarders use water carriers.

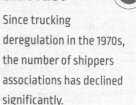

stat fact

Since trucking deregulation in the 1970s, the number of shippers associations has declined significantly.

▶ *Import-export broker.* These people are facilitators for importers and exporters (import brokers are also referred to as customhouse brokers). Import-export brokers interface with U.S. Customs, other government agencies, international carriers, and other companies and organizations that are involved in international freight transportation.

▶ *Agricultural truck broker.* Generally small and operating in one area of the country, unregulated agricultural truck brokers arrange motor carrier service for exempt agricultural products.

▶ *Shippers associations.* Shippers associations are exempt, nonprofit, cooperative organizations formed by shippers to reduce transportation costs by pooling shipments. Shippers associations operate in a manner very similar to that of freight forwarders, but their services are limited to their members and are not available to the general public.

In a perfect world, of course, each entity in the industry would handle its traditional role and that's all. However, the transportation industry is changing so rapidly that once-distinctive lines have blurred. Also, it's quite common for a successful freight broker to expand his or her business by creating subsidiaries or additional companies that offer other freight services.

Plus, while it's not possible to fully automate a freight brokerage business, technology and specialized software (from companies like DAT Solutions, LLC, www.dat.com/products/broker-tms) are currently being used heavily by freight brokers of all sizes, so they can work much more efficiently when it comes to managing operations, accounting, document management, and analytics. Thus, a successful freight broker must understand how to best utilize the specialized technology that's at their disposal to remain highly competitive.

A key issue, say industry experts, is that legal definitions have not been challenged recently, so freight forwarders may be acting as brokers, and brokers may assume the role of freight forwarders. In the event of a cargo claim or nonpayment of bills, problems can

▶ A Truck by Any Other Name

The term "truck" is an umbrella word covering a wide range of equipment. Among the types of trucks you'll need to be familiar with are:

- ▶ *Dry vans* (non-refrigerated semitrailers)
- ▶ *Refrigerated semitrailers* (or "reefers")
- ▶ *Flats or flatbeds* (flat trailers built to handle heavy loads such as metal and machinery)
- ▶ *Liquid tankers* (trailers designed to carry liquid or fine bulk materials)
- ▶ *Ragtops* (canvas-covered, boxlike trailers)
- ▶ *Containers* (shipping containers used for freight carried on ships or trains)
- ▶ *Air-ride* (trailers built to reduce road shock and designed to carry fragile items)

arise when a company holds multiple authorities. The question becomes: Who was wearing what hat and when?

Clearly, pushing the proverbial envelope when it comes to services and operations has some definite risks, and you'll want to carefully consider all of your options when setting up your business. If you're new to the industry, nothing replaces the need for specialized training and real-world experience prior to working in this field as the operator of a freight brokerage. Without proper training and some real-world experience, you're much more apt to make costly mistakes and destroy business relationships.

How They Started

Ask a class of first graders what they want to be when they grow up, and you'll likely hear things like doctor, firefighter, police officer, superhero,

tip

As a freight broker, you'll build your company on repeat business. If you do a good job, you'll rarely have a one-time customer. Most shippers have routine, repetitive shipments that move around the country on a predictable schedule. As you become familiar with these shipments, they become easier to handle. To establish loyal customers and generate repeat business, not only must you master the skills related to becoming a skilled freight broker, you'll also need to develop and polish your sales, problem solving, time management, and organizational and interpersonal communication skills.

or lawyer; it's highly unlikely anyone will say "freight broker." So how do successful freight brokers get into the business?

Bill Tucker's brokerage in Cherry Hill, New Jersey, has employed three generations of his family. His father founded the firm in 1961 by purchasing one of the few broker's licenses still operating at the time. Years later, Tucker was working in the computer industry when his father passed away unexpectedly. At first, he and his mother decided to sell the business rather than shut it down, so he helped run it while looking for a buyer. But after several months without a realistic offer, Tucker decided that he wanted the company for himself. He worked out a deal to buy the company from his mother, and now his own sons work for him. "I've never regretted it because it has been a great business," he says.

After holding a variety of jobs in the transportation industry, Cathy Davis started MCD Transportation, Inc. as a consulting and commissioned sales agency in 1986, and obtained brokerage authority in 1991. After she passed away in 2002, her daughters took over the Smyrna, Tennessee-based company.

▶ Working 9 to 5

While it's certainly possible to start a freight brokerage as a part-time business and gradually expand it into a full-time operation, this approach is not recommended. This is not a business where problems or issues can wait. You need to be accessible to your customers during regular business hours and often after normal business hours as well. If you're not available to answer a question, solve a problem, or quote a rate when a shipper needs information, for example, they'll likely take their business elsewhere.

There's also the image issue to consider. Whether it's a valid perception or not, many people view part-time businesses as hobbies, and their operators as less than professional. Many shippers are not going to trust their shipments to a part-time freight broker.

If you need more income than your business will generate in its early days, consider operating a full-time brokerage with a part-time job on the side—but be sure the hours you work at the other job won't interfere with your brokerage. Try to schedule that work for nights and weekends. Alternatively, consider becoming an agent for a brokerage firm, instead of operating your own freight brokerage.

Chuck Andrews started his business in Indianapolis in 1993. Having spent his entire professional life working for trucking companies and railroads, he found the brokerage business tremendously appealing. "Out of all the transportation operations, a brokerage operation is very clean," he says. "By that, I mean it's basically a 7:30 A.M. to 5 P.M. operation. Very seldom do you have problems occur after that. Your operation runs Monday through Friday. When you're on the trucking side of it, you have all the problems. If a guy blows a tire, he's calling somebody at one or two o'clock in the morning to get money to fix it. With brokers, it's our concern—we want the freight moving on schedule—but it's not our problem, because the driver is going to call his dispatcher or his company."

For 18 years, Ron Williamson worked as a corporate traffic manager and director of distribution for several major corporations. He also had experience with a railroad and a transportation-consulting firm. Finally, when he could no longer resist the entrepreneurial urge, he started his own brokerage firm in 1981, based in Bloomingdale, Illinois, and has since founded two trucking companies as well.

Specialist or Generalist?

As a broker, you have the opportunity to handle many types of freight. You may opt to simply handle general commodity freight—materials that are typically easy to handle and don't require any special attention. However, you might want to develop some expertise in areas such as heavy equipment, oversized loads, perishable commodities, or even hazardous materials. Becoming an expert at coordinating the transportation of specialized goods could easily allow you to charge premium rates for your services and make it easier for you to find clients (shippers).

Don't limit your specialization plan to the commonly accepted areas. Instead, find your own niche. Tucker, for example, does some interesting work for retailers. One major national chain hires his company to handle the distribution of point-of-sale promotional displays that have to be delivered to hundreds of stores on the same day. It's a move that's important but not frequent enough for the retailer to maintain the required expertise

aha!

If you're working with a carrier or broker now and are planning to quit in order to start your own brokerage, don't assume the customers you have a good relationship with will automatically follow you. It may happen, but if you're counting on that customer for early revenue, you could be in for a rude awakening.

in-house. Other big businesses use Tucker's company to manage shipments related to store openings and closings.

Who's Minding the Store?

Even following deregulation, the transportation industry comes under the regulation of a number of different agencies. The least-regulated cargo is intrastate freight—shipments moving within the borders of a single state. That freight is regulated under the laws of the particular state and is also typically regulated by the state's department of transportation, department of business and professional regulation, and/or the department of revenue and taxation.

For interstate shipments—shipments moving between states—the key regulatory agency prior to 1995 was the Interstate Commerce Commission (ICC), an independent agency created by Congress in 1887 to regulate commercial activity crossing state lines. The ICC was created in response to turmoil within the railroad industry, and came about after an 1886 Supreme Court ruling that said states could not regulate interstate railroads, which effectively shifted the burden of regulation to the federal government.

The commission initially possessed limited regulatory powers, but by the early 1950s its jurisdiction extended to all types of surface transportation vehicles and channels. The agency was criticized for regulatory excess and setting artificially high transportation and shipping rates. By the early 1980s, deregulation of transportation industries had stripped the ICC of most of its authority to set rates. In 1995, Congress abolished the ICC and created a Surface Transportation Board (STB) within the Department of Transportation (DOT). The responsibility of the DOT is to perform the small number of regulatory tasks that had remained with the ICC. Today, the primary agencies that oversee motor freight transportation are the STB, DOT, and the Federal Motor Carrier Safety Administration (FMCSA).

Do You Have What It Takes?

This is not a business for the faint of heart or a shy person who is happiest shuffling papers behind closed office doors or within their cubical. However, courage and an extroverted personality alone won't guarantee you a successful freight brokerage either. According to Davis, "Anyone involved in operations needs to be able to handle stress, make quick decisions, handle multiple tasks, have a good phone voice, and develop top-notch communication skills. It's also good to possess some general business knowledge." You not only need to understand the freight industry, you must also appreciate the business demands your customers face.

Andrews agrees that communication skills and a solid foundation in the industry are important for brokers. You need to be able to speak industry jargon to demonstrate your knowledge. "The worst thing you could do is call a shipper and start fumbling on the phone," he says. "He's never going to give you any freight because he's going to know right away that you have no knowledge of the business, and he would not trust his goods being moved with you."

Williamson says you've got to be "a good all-around person." That means being comfortable with the financial side, the sales side, and the operations side. Understanding how to leverage technology and specialized software designed for use by freight brokers has also become increasingly more important within the past five years.

The TIA's Voltmann says, "The future for intermediaries is very bright as asset-owning carriers concentrate on what they do best, and shippers concentrate on their core competencies. Shippers and carriers need the innovation and expertise intermediaries provide. The result will be continued improvements, which will mean more choices for consumers and lower costs."

Start Your Own Freight Brokerage Business is an easy-to-read resource that will introduce you to this business opportunity. However, it's only a starting point if you opt to pursue this type of career path. How you proceed should depend on your goals, financial resources, existing education, the amount of additional job-specific training, and general business education you're able and willing to acquire, as well as your willingness to build your own business from scratch over time (as opposed to working for an existing freight brokerage business, potentially as an agent or as an employee).

If you opt to pursue starting your own freight brokerage business, one of the first things you'll want to do is obtain proper training. Simply by visiting your favorite internet search engine, such as Google (www.google.com) or Yahoo! (www.yahoo.com), enter the phrase "freight broker training" within the search field, to learn about the various schools and organizations that offer this type of training.

As you'll discover, you can participate in online-based classes at your own pace, or obtain instruction in person within a traditional classroom setting. Depending on which training program you choose, the cost will range from just under $500 to several thousand dollars, and the time commitment required will typically be between one week and several months.

Some of the organizations that offer the specialized training that you ultimately need include:

▶ *Brooke Transportation Training Solutions* (www.brooketraining.com). Offers classroom training in multiple cities across the United States, as well as an online program that can be done from home. The course price starts at $2,495.00 for the intensive, five-day (40-hour) program, although a two-week (80-hour) course is also offered that's designed specifically for people looking to start their own brokerage business as opposed to working as an agent or as an employee for a broker.

▶ *Ed2go* (www.ed2go.com). Offers a six month, classroom-based course (in conjunction with Palm Beach State College), which starts at $1,895.00.

▶ *FBC Freight Brokerage Course* (http://freightbrokerscourse.com/products/freight-broker-training/). Offers home study and online-based programs ranging in price from $99 to $699.

▶ *TIA Delivers* (www.tianet.org). Offers a home study course.

Optionally earning a Certified Transportation Broker accreditation will provide you with the textbook knowledge needed to establish yourself in this industry. However, absolutely nothing can replace the need for real-world training and experience, which you can only obtain from actually working for an established freight brokerage, or by working in other aspects of the ground transportation/freight industry.

While this work experience is optional prior to starting your own freight brokerage business (or becoming an agent), it's an extremely savvy business practice to acquire at least some industry-related, real-world experience before attempting to launch your own freight brokerage business.

Beyond the industry-specific training and knowledge that's required, running any type of business requires the business operator to juggle many responsibilities, and wear many different proverbial hats, so you'll also want to develop general business and bookkeeping experience. In other words, you need to be able to efficiently handle the core responsibilities of being a general business operator.

Thus, taking general business, marketing, and technology-related courses will help you develop and fine-tune the core business and marketing skills you'll need. If you're

▶ Further Your Education Online

General business classes can be taken online, at your own pace, from a wide range of accredited institutions. It's also possible to participate in free, online-based classes from iTunes U, for example, by downloading the free iTunes U app onto your Mac, iPhone, or iPad. The iTunes U app is available from the App Store. Once you launch the free app, you will be able to browse an extensive course catalog, choose which classes to participate in, and then sign up and participate in each selected class.

University of Phoenix [www.phoenix.edu/colleges_divisions/business.html] is just one example of an online, accredited institution that offers fee-based business classes. Open Culture [www.openculture.com] and Alison Learning [http://alison.com], however, are other resources for participating in free, online business classes that range from accounting, human resources, operations management, leadership skills development, marketing, business writing, and negotiation to business communications, sales management, and fundamentals of business law.

not technologically savvy, learning how to operate a computer and use industry-specific software, as well as general business and bookkeeping software, will all ultimately be essential if you opt to launch your own freight brokerage business.

It's also essential that you develop strong written and verbal communication skills, since you'll continuously be interacting with other people in person, in writing, via email, and over the phone. At the same time, becoming a savvy negotiator will help you. These skills can be acquired through the use of self-help courses, or by participating in evening classes, community college classes, or online classes, for example.

Before Becoming a Freight Broker or Agent, Get the Proper Training

Reading *Start Your Own Freight Brokerage Business* is a wonderful first step toward obtaining the knowledge and skills needed to start a freight brokerage business or becoming an agent for an existing business. However, it is just a first step.

After reading this book, if you decide this is a career path you want to pursue, seriously consider investing the time and money needed to acquire the proper training and education. This can be done by taking a live, hands-on training program that requires between 40 and

80 hours in a classroom environment, or it can be done at your own pace, by participating in an online-based training course.

As you'll soon discover, the people who want to acquire the most comprehensive training begin by completing an online training program, and then take a live, hands-on training program, so they can interact with and learn from experienced instructors in person.

When it comes to finding a training program, you have many options to choose from. One option is Brooke Transportation Training Solutions (www.brooketraining. com/our-courses). Founded by Jeff Roach, this organization offers both an online training program, as well as 40- and 80-hour live training programs that are taught in multiple cities throughout the country.

Roach has spent his entire adult life working in various aspects of the ground transportation industry and for the past two decades has operated a highly successful freight brokerage business called Brooke Transportation Services, which is based in the Dallas/Fort Worth area.

It was back in 2001, when he was looking for a training program for his own employees but could not find a good one, that he decided to create Brooke Transportation Training Solutions and began developing an ever-evolving and extremely comprehensive training program, which is now available to the public.

Over the years, tens of thousands of students have graduated from Roach's training programs and have gone on to pursue their own successful careers operating a freight brokerage business or working as an agent for an established company.

In this interview, Jeff Roach shares valuable information about how to acquire the education and training needed in order to operate a successful freight brokerage business or become an agent for an existing freight broker.

"When I started in this business, unless you already knew someone working within it, you didn't know what it was. The concept of a freight brokerage or freight broker agent was simply unheard of, even though these companies existed. What I have seen over the past few years is that knowledge about this type of business has become much more mainstream. It used to be people who got into the freight brokerage business were migrating from the trucking business, for example, because they were the only ones who knew about this opportunity. Today, people are graduating from high school or college and are choosing this as a career path," explained Roach.

"Today, companies in many different industries, and of all sizes, are using freight brokers or third-party logistics companies, which are basically the same thing. When I first started in this business and had to call on shippers, I often had to explain what a freight broker was. Today, this is no longer the case. Not only do all shippers know about freight brokers, most shippers now rely heavily on them," added Roach.

As in any industry, technology is changing the way people do business. While there are many technology-based tools that can be used by freight brokerage businesses to automate some aspects of their work, Roach does not see technology replacing the need for freight brokers any time soon.

"Over the next three to five years, I think there will be new software and technologies introduced that will handle more of the tasks and decision making that's currently done by freight brokers. So it's important for people entering this field to understand how to use technology and to stay up-to-date on these latest advancements. Technology will help with efficiencies and asset utilizations, plus make it possible to make decisions faster," said Roach.

Many freight brokerage businesses operate throughout the United States, and there's a lot of existing competition in this field. However, Roach strongly believes that tremendous opportunities still exist for people first breaking into this field.

"There has never been a better opportunity than there is right now for freight brokerage businesses. If you look at transportation stocks, for example, they're hitting an all-time high. With the new Republican-led U.S. government, starting in early 2017, there is going to be a huge infrastructure building program within the United States. I think we are at the beginning of a renaissance period as far as it being the best time ever, in the history of the world, for transportation companies, transportation services, brokers, and agents," explained Roach. "Companies in many industries, and of all sizes, are investing heavily in transportation and logistics. I see tremendous opportunities existing and growing in many areas of the ground transportation industry."

When asked to describe the ideal student for one of Brooke Transportation Training Solutions's programs, Roach responded, "Everyone needs to enter this field with realistic expectations. This is not a career path for someone who does not like to work. This is a career for people who like to wake up early and spend their entire day solving problems and developing creative solutions for evolving problems. It never stops. You make a living in this business by solving problems.

"When operating a freight brokerage business, there is no such thing as running it on autopilot. You have to be the kind of person who loves to solve problems. Each and every day, you are going to be solving problems for shippers and carriers. Thus, you have to enter this industry with the right expectations and the right attitude. It's not for the faint of heart.

"There are many different personality types that do well working in this industry, but you need to understand that you're literally going to be sitting in front of a computer and on the phone every day, from morning to night. You're going to be continuously communicating with shippers, traffic managers, dispatchers, drivers, and other logistics companies, for example. Again, this career is for people who love to work hard and solve problems.

"In terms of core skills and prior education, I have seen plenty of people with little formal education succeed once they've acquired the proper training to operate a freight brokerage business or become an agent. I have also seen people with college degrees succeed. This industry is open to everyone, as long as they're willing to work hard and do what they say they're going to do. The last thing I am going to do is put restraints on people by telling them they're not an ideal candidate for this industry," said Roach.

After years of being an instructor and training thousands of individuals to operate their own freight brokerage businesses, Roach says that he can look at a new class of students and pick out who will likely become the most successful by pinpointing one certain trait.

"The person who has overcome the most adversity in their life and did not quit will be the person who is the most successful working in this field. This is a business that takes that type of character—someone who is not going to quit when things get difficult or stressful. This is a job where you are putting out fires and solving problems. It never stops. You can't be the type of person who gives up easily. You need to be the type of person who gets knocked down and who gets right back up again.

"Someone who has encountered great setbacks in their life and has overcome them will typically do much better in this type of work than someone who has had everything handed to them. There is nothing easy about this career path. If anyone says working in a freight brokerage business, or operating one, is easy work, they are lying to you," added Roach.

For people who have no previous experience working in the freight, shipping, or ground transportation industry, Roach believes that the very best way to get started is to invest the required 40 to 80 hours in order to obtain training.

"You will learn what works and what doesn't work. Operating a freight brokerage business, or working as an agent, is not the type of job that requires you to pass a test, get a license, and then get started. There are a lot of excellent courses out there. Participate in one," said Roach.

"I am 100 percent sure that what's covered within our courses is the most accurate, most timely, and most necessary information someone needs. We help people break into this industry with the knowledge they need to become successful.

"Before you spend any money to obtain a freight brokerage license and acquire a surety bond that could cost thousands of dollars, obtain the right training, determine the best path for you to personally follow, and then decide how to proceed next in terms of in what capacity you'll enter this industry. It might make financial sense for you to first become an agent, as opposed to launching your own freight brokerage business. Make intelligent decisions based on knowledge and coaching," explained Roach.

Not everyone chooses to open their own freight brokerage business and wants to take on that added financial responsibility. Roach stated, "If you choose to become an agent first, upon completing one of our training programs, we will personally introduce you to established freight brokers looking to hire agents immediately, so after participating in a 40- or 80-hour course, you could land a really good job working for a broker, for example. Start with good training, and then choose a career path in this industry based on your risk tolerance and financial situation."

In terms of choosing between an online-based or live training program, Roach explained that everyone learns best in a different way. "If you want to work at your own pace, and learn every little detail about everything, an online course may be best suited for you. However, if you want to take a more hands-on approach to your training, participate in a live course, where you're sitting in front of your instructors. Our online course is interactive, and offers everything you could possibly want to know about this business. It's one of the highest rated programs offered by Education To Go (www.ed2go.com), and it's available through 2,000 colleges and universities in multiple languages. For people who can't travel, the online course is perfect," said Roach.

According to Roach, the live classes are extremely hands-on in terms of their approach. Not only do the live classes explain how to make sales calls to potential shippers, but during the class, students actually make the calls, and then get critiqued on their performance. He said, "People come to our live course because they want hands-on experience, not just textbook knowledge."

For those students with the most time, financial resources, and schedule flexibility, in order to obtain the maximum level of training, Roach recommends completing the online course offered by Brooke Transportation Training Solutions and then participating in the two week (80-hour) live training program. For someone looking to set up and operate their own brokerage, this is the best solution for acquiring the comprehensive knowledge and hands-on experience you will need to be successful. "Hands-on, live training is not something that can be emulated online," said Roach.

On the final day of training, representatives from a handful of companies that offer resources and software for operating a freight brokerage business make presentations. "Someone can leave the training with just about everything they need, plus have a clear understanding of what the next steps should be for them," added Roach. "If you want to become an agent, established brokers will come to the final class and be on hand for recruiting purposes. Graduates from the training need to decide what path they want to take. This will determine the steps they need to take next, and what their immediate financial obligations will be to get up and running."

Early in his interview, Roach stressed that someone interested in becoming a broker or agent should enter this field with realistic expectations. The best way to develop these expectations is to work with a trainer or coach, or to spend some time working for another company. "Listen and learn from someone with experience and who wants you to become successful. My whole goal is to teach people how to go down this road with realistic expectations. I will present information and answer every question that's posed to me, but I will never sell this career path on anyone," said Roach.

He added, "The biggest mistake people make going into this field is that they initially spend a lot of money that they don't need to spend. For example, they go out and acquire a license and a bond for their business before they've even decided to establish a freight brokerage business. Depending on the path someone chooses to take, these expenses might not be necessary. I recommend that someone invest in the proper training or coaching first. Then, based on the information you obtain, decide what else you want or need to invest in.

"Keep in mind, the premium in this business is not finding trucks. The premium and challenge is finding shippers. People come to me wanting to become a broker, because they already know several people who own trucks, or have contacts in the ground transportation industry. That's great, but what you need as a broker are shippers to work with. Training will teach you how to find potential shippers, make sales calls like a pro, and how to build lasting business relationships. I truly believe that Brooke Transportation Training Solutions is the very best in the business when it comes to training our students on how to make successful sales calls to shippers," said Roach.

Developing core business skills, having an outgoing personality, and learning the ins and outs of working as a freight broker are all essential. According to Roach, what's equally important is that someone entering this field also has integrity and character. "It's all about building trust and doing what you say you're going to do, when you say you're going to do it. Without trust and relationships, you have nothing in this business."

stat fact

Trucking accounts for 81 percent of the nation's freight bill, and trucks move approximately 67 percent (by weight) of the nation's freight.

The online-based training program from Brooke Transportation Training Solutions is priced at $1,695 (as of early 2017). The live, five-day (40-hour) Freight Brokerage Basic course, offered in a wide range of cities, is priced at $2,495, while the Freight Broker Advanced Course (an additional 40 hours) is priced at $3,995. Financing is available for the online course, and 100 percent financial aid is available for qualified vets through the VA Chapter 31 Program (www.brooketraining. com/veterans).

In addition to the Brooke Transportation Training Solutions website, which offers information about the company's training programs, Roach publishes the free *Freight Broker Training Information Blog* (http://freight-broker-info.blogspot. com), which he continuously updates with articles, advice, and information about useful resources. Plus, the company is active on Facebook (www.facebook.com/ BrookeTransportationTrainingSolutionsLLC) and LinkedIn (www.linkedin.com/in/ jeffery-roach-9a427153).

"Between the website, our blog, Facebook, and LinkedIn, we do everything we can to get the best information and resources out there for people who are already in the industry and for people who want to get into this industry," concluded Roach.

He recommends the TIA (Transportation Intermediaries Association, www.tianet. org) as another excellent resource for someone interested in learning more about this field. However, he suggests waiting to join this organization until after you've opened your own freight brokerage business, because the annual membership fees for this industry association are expensive.

What Does the Business Require?

The dissolution of the Interstate Commerce Commission, and other aspects of transportation deregulation, has left many industry players confused about what is regulated and what is not. This chapter addresses the regulatory and practical requirements of starting and running a freight brokerage, although state and federal laws and regulations are continuously changing.

Freight brokers must register with the Federal Motor Carrier Safety Administration (FMCSA). This is not a complicated process. Essentially, you must file an application (Form OP-1) and pay a filing fee, obtain a $75,000 surety bond or establish a trust fund, and designate agents for service of legal process. The registration will remain valid as long as these requirements continue to be met. Keep in mind, this is something that must be done by the freight brokerage business, not an individual freight broker or agent.

The surety bond or trust fund is evidence of financial responsibility. This means you must demonstrate that you have access to that amount of liquid assets to meet your obligations and pay any potential claims. You can either use your own resources or contract with a bonding company. Evidence of a surety bond must be filed using Form BMC 84; evidence of a trust fund with a financial institution must be filed using Form BMC 85.

Designation of process agents means that for each state in which you have offices or in which you write contracts, you must file a designation of person on whom court process may be served.

When your application is approved, you'll receive a permit with a Motor Carrier (MC) number from the FMCSA that is your authority to operate as a freight broker within the United States. Beyond the regulations that govern your particular operation, when you act on behalf of a person bound by law or FMCSA regulations as to the transmittal of bills or payments, you must also abide by the laws or regulations that apply to that person.

In addition to federal requirements, you'll need whatever business licenses and/or operational permits that are required by your local and state governments.

Check with your local planning and zoning department or city/county business license department to find out what you need and what is involved in obtaining these licenses and/or permits. For example, you may need an occupational license or permit issued by your city or county, a fire department permit if you are in a commercial location and/or open to the public, and/or a sign permit.

Education and Experience

Prior to opening your own freight brokerage business, it's an excellent strategy to first work for another company within the industry—either for a shipper, a carrier, or both. The more real-world industry experience you have, in addition to industry-specific training, the better off you'll be. Through real-world experience, you'll not only gain technical expertise, you'll also make contacts that are critical to success in this business.

Cathy Davis entered the industry as an inventory control clerk for a river terminal, and then spent time working in sales for motor and air freight carriers. "I was fortunate to have been mentored by the owner of the carrier I worked for," she recalled.

warning

Don't try to get around the law. Penalties for evasion of regulation by motor carriers and brokers include a civil penalty of $200 for the first violation and at least $250 for a subsequent violation.

Her consulting business gave her the opportunity to learn even more about being a broker. She was an agent for brokers before becoming one herself, and that gave her both hands-on experience and an opportunity to build her reputation within the industry.

"I highly recommend this startup method with total disclosure of intent and a legal agreement," she said. Later, she earned the Certified Transportation Broker designation through the Transportation Intermediaries Association (TIA), as did her daughters before they took over the Smyrna, Tennessee-based company.

Similarly, Chuck Andrews, who is based in Indianapolis, held senior positions with a major LTL carrier, was president of a truckload (TL) carrier, and has worked in railroad operations. "My whole background leading up to forming my freight brokerage company has all been in transportation," he says.

Davis believed new brokers need "a strong sales background, good business advisors, and a desire for continuing education."

Building Carrier Relationships

How can you build strong, positive relationships with carriers? "Pay on time, and pay reasonable rates," said Davis. Of course, she added, having "driver-friendly" freight is a positive aspect, and communication is critical.

"We use a load-matching service to help find carriers, but also network with members in various organizations. We consider the carrier to be a customer and extend the same degree of professionalism to a transaction with them as we do with shippers."

Establishing and building relationships with carriers and shippers will likely be your biggest startup challenge. "Because of brokers who have gone out of business (owing carriers money), truckers are very careful about who they do business with," says Andrews. "If you do not have a history with that trucking company, he's not going to be very aggressive in wanting to haul your load because he doesn't know if he's going to get paid or not. Even though you have signed all the papers and you've got your surety bond, he's going to be leery until he gets that first check from you."

While there are services for brokers that are designed to help you easily find carriers, it's almost entirely up to you to seek out, negotiate with, and develop relationships with shippers. After all, without shippers willing to pay you for your services, you have no business.

It's a problem that only time can solve. "It took us quite a few years to build up our business," Andrews says. "We currently have close to 7,000 truckers under contract to move our freight." When he adds a new trucker, he presents himself as a reliable, professional

▶ Bond . . . Surety Bond

Many people do not have a clear understanding of what a bond actually does. Basically, it is an amount of money that you post to guarantee that you will do something you've promised to do. Probably the most common way you hear the term "bond" used is in criminal cases. When someone is arrested and charged with a crime, he or she can put up an amount of money (or something else of value) to guarantee an appearance in court. If the person shows up as promised, the money is returned; if he or she is a no show, the money is forfeited.

Because many people do not have the cash on hand to post the full amount of a required bond, they turn to a bonding company. The bonding company charges a percentage of the total bond to put up whatever amount of money is required. The money the bonding company collects is a fee and is not refundable. In addition to charging the fee, the bonding company may also ask you to post collateral, such as real estate or equipment.

Here's where the confusion on bonds often occurs: A bond is not insurance you purchase; it is the collateral for a promise. And if you use a bonding company, you are still ultimately responsible for the total amount of the bond, not just the fee you paid to the company.

In the case of a freight broker, the surety bond guarantees that you will meet all your contractual obligations to your customers, and that you can pay any claims immediately. If you use a bonding company and that company pays any claims on your behalf you must repay the company, usually within 90 days. If you fail to repay, and have posted collateral, you will likely lose that collateral.

broker by sending an information package that includes information on the company, as well as a listing of key personnel, bank information, and carrier references. "The hard part is getting that first load moved and then being able to build on that for your credit references."

warning

Be sure to fully check the references and credentials of all the carriers you use, before you ever give them the first load. If you fail to do so and a problem occurs, you could find yourself responsible for the damages.

It's important to understand the economics of the trucking business when you negotiate payment terms with your carriers. In the past, ICC regulations dictated that freight bills be paid within seven days; today, since deregulation, that is negotiable. But carriers operate on very narrow margins and pay most of their expenses on a given load before they ever pick up the load, so cash flow is as critical to them as it is to the broker.

Some brokers would prefer not to have to pay the carrier until they get paid themselves, and while that would be a safe approach for the broker, you won't find carriers very enthusiastic about it.

"Carriers take the stand that the reason they are using a broker is so they don't have to do credit checks on the customers, or do the sales and service that we provide," says Cherry Hill, New Jersey-based freight broker Bill Tucker. "It's one of the reasons the carriers will sell to you a little lower than they would bill the shipper direct. The carriers are saying, 'You handle the credit for your customer base and you pay me whether you get paid or not.' It just keeps it simpler and cleaner."

Tucker notes that there may be times, such as with high-volume shippers or a special seasonal situation, when the billing can escalate rapidly, and the broker and carrier agree to share the financial risk. But those types of contract clauses are the exceptions. Tucker explained, "I would say that in 99 percent of the transactions, the broker does the collections and pays the trucker every penny owed."

Banking On Your Banker

Solid banking relationships are critical for brokers. Andrews says it's not unusual for a new broker to need a line of credit in the range of $250,000 to $500,000 in order to be able to pay carriers before being paid by the shippers.

"If you don't pay the trucks in a timely fashion, they won't haul your freight. If you have nobody to haul your freight, you have no business," he says. "Other than getting your licensing and insurance, setting up with a good banker should probably be at the top of your to-do list."

Of course, you don't want to walk empty-handed into a bank you've never done business with and ask for a major line of credit. "You have to know your banker really well. Go in with a business plan. It also helps if you have been doing business with that bank and they already know you," said Andrews. "You have to have an excellent credit record, because—as a broker—you have no assets for them to come after."

► Start Me Up

The following table will give you an idea of the necessary startup expenses for a freight brokerage business. Where your operation falls within the ranges depends on whether you start as a homebased business or in a commercial location, and whether you hire employees right away or do everything yourself in the beginning. The suggested operating capital should be enough to cover the first three months of operation and must be sufficient to cover paying carriers before you are paid by shippers.

Keep in mind, there are also licensing fees that new freight brokerage companies need to pay upfront. You can, however, forego most of these upfront costs by becoming an agent who works for a freight brokerage company.

Advertising/marketing	$500 – $1,500+
Equipment	$6,000 – $25,000
Insurance (first quarter)	$700 – $1,400+
Licenses/tax deposits	$200 – $400
Payroll	$0 – $5,000+
Professional services	$200 – $1000
Rent	$0 – $5,000
Specialized freight broker software	$300+ per month
Suggested operating capital	$5,000 – $300,000 (cash or line of credit)
Supplies	$300 – $500
Training and education	$1000 – $5000
Utilities/phone service	$100 – $300+

Put together a package that clearly demonstrates to the bank that you are not a credit risk, so they can easily see how they'll benefit by establishing a line of credit for your business.

In these days of banking mergers and acquisitions, along with personnel turnover, it's a good idea to have relationships with more than one bank. If you have a single line of credit with one bank and that bank gets sold, you could find your line of credit getting canceled through no fault of your own. Or if you have a strong relationship with a loan officer who gets promoted, transferred, or changes jobs, you may find the new loan officer not as receptive to your needs. Protect yourself by making sure you always have a financial backup to turn to.

Those Critical Customers

Certainly you need strong relationships with your carriers and bankers, but the most essential outside element of your business is your customer base—the shippers. Though you'll do a certain amount of cold calling as you market your business, hopefully most of your customers will come through referrals, contacts, and networking. You can use your network to get in the door, but remember, this is about business, not just about friendship. "Just because you know someone doesn't mean they are going to give you the business if your pricing isn't competitive," says Andrews.

Of course, there's more involved than just pricing. Communication is essential. Let customers (shippers) know what's happening with their shipments every step of the way. Andrews says this means almost-daily contact. Shippers need the comfort of knowing when their freight is moving as scheduled and the opportunity to react appropriately if it isn't. Most shippers can deal with mechanical, weather, or traffic delays as long as they know about them. Don't let them find out from their customers that shipments weren't delivered as scheduled; let them know ahead of time that, for whatever reason, the truck isn't going to make it, and when they can expect delivery.

Record-Keeping Requirements

The Code of Federal Regulations is very specific about what types of records you must maintain. While you may keep a master list of shippers and carriers to avoid repeating the information, you are required to keep a record of each transaction. That record must show:

- ▶ The name and address of the consignor (shipper)
- ▶ The name, address, and registration number of the originating motor carrier
- ▶ The bill of lading (see the Glossary) or freight bill number
- ▶ The amount of compensation received by the broker for the brokerage service performed and the name of the payer
- ▶ A description of any non-brokerage service performed in connection with each shipment or other activity, the amount of compensation received for the service, and the name of the payer
- ▶ The amount of any freight charges collected by the broker and the date of payment to the carrier

Industry-specific software, such as what's available from DAT Solutions, LLC (www.dat.com/resources/product-sheets/dat-keypoint-core-features), can help you organize, manage information, and automate some tasks associated with being a freight broker. Using specialized software will help you become far more efficient than if you rely on spreadsheets and documents created using Microsoft Office applications, for example.

You must keep these records for a period of three years, and each party to a particular transaction has a right to review the records relating to that transaction.

See Figure 2–1 on page 27 for a list of the key elements of a successful freight brokerage business.

warning

Even though your contract will prohibit it, you may occasionally work with a carrier that will approach your client directly. This is bad business, and it's likely that a carrier operating with such a lack of integrity won't be in business long. Nonetheless, be aware that it can happen, and if you find out about it, be prepared to take the appropriate legal steps, including cease and desist orders and suing for lost revenue.

▶ Be Careful What You Say

There may be situations when you're with other brokers—or even shippers and carriers—and the conversation centers around customers you have in common. Protect the privacy of your customers and the confidentiality of their businesses. Not only is this a sound professional business practice, but you are prohibited by law from disclosing information to an unrelated party that may be used to the detriment of the shipper or consignee.

Golden Rules for Transportation Intermediaries

1. Know the company you are dealing with. Establish criteria that must be met by the parties with whom you will have a business transaction. Create a checklist, and use it every time you establish a new relationship. (Specialized software can help you automate this process.)

2. Create a procedure for tracking the performance of the companies with which you establish a relationship. Review performance often. (Specialized software can help you automate this process.)

3. Take action early if things begin to go wrong. Line staff must communicate recurring problems to management.

4. Make sure there are no surprises! Be willing to convey why you need information so people can be supportive and participatory.

5. Provide load confirmation in a timely manner—15 to 30 minutes. Minimum information: consignor/consignee; origin/destination; commodity; value; rate; pickup and delivery schedule; pallet considerations; and any special requirements. Immediately return Rate Agreement.

6. Immediately convey "change" information. Time is of the essence. People can generally accommodate changes if given enough notice.

7. Be a role model in developing cooperative service attitudes. Provide proper training to your employees so they too can be effective problem solvers.

8. Provide accurate invoices promptly. Provide Proof of Deliveries as requested. (Specialized software can help you automate this process.)

9. Carriers and intermediaries should provide 24-hour access to each other.

10. Appreciate the skills, experience, and professionalism brought to each transaction by all involved parties. Express this appreciation sincerely and frequently.

11. Be straightforward in all contractual and financial matters.

These principles were established during the Joint Trust Forum between Transportation Brokers Conference of America and National Association of Small Trucking Companies in Nashville, Tennessee, in 1994.

FIGURE 2–1: **Golden Rules for Transportation Intermediaries**

Operations

The basic concept of freight brokering is pretty simple: A shipper (or consignor, as they're sometimes referred to) calls you with a load. You complete your own internal paperwork and check with your carriers to see who has a vehicle available. If you already have a relationship with a carrier, you fax or email them an addendum to your basic contract that describes this particular load and the rate. If the carrier agrees, the company's representative signs the document and sends it back. (If you don't already have a relationship with the carrier, you'll need to set up a carrier/broker agreement before you finalize the deal on the first shipment.)

Next, the carrier dispatches the driver. It's a good idea to require that the driver call you (or use your online tracking system) to confirm that the load has been picked up, and again when it has been delivered.

After the shipment has been delivered, the carrier will send you an invoice and the original bill of lading. You invoice your customer (the shipper), pay the trucker, and then, ideally, do the whole thing again with another shipment.

A successful freight broker will ultimately be handling this process simultaneously on behalf of multiple shippers and/or handle multiple shipments simultaneously on behalf of a single shipper. Thus, it's essential that you always keep track of all relevant details that are pertinent to each job.

Facts on File

When you arrange a shipment, you'll need information from both the shipper and the carrier. Much of this information should be kept on file in your office. Again, this is something specialized software can help you manage.

Shipper Information

Maintaining detailed information on shippers helps you provide better customer service, and saves you from having to take the time to ask the same questions with each shipment. Keep the following information:

- ▶ Company name
- ▶ Physical address
- ▶ Billing address, if different from physical address
- ▶ All telephone numbers (cell phones, voice mail, fax, pagers), including any toll-free numbers
- ▶ All email addresses
- ▶ Contact people (including traffic and shipping managers, freight payable person, and anyone else you may deal with)
- ▶ Type of freight shipped (machinery, produce, chemicals, etc.)

► Type of equipment (trucks) required

► Pallet exchange requirements

► Other special requirements

► Any other pickup information you require (such as warehouse locations or other distribution points)

This information will not change frequently, but you should always make sure you have current information. Immediately update anything you find out about during the course of handling a shipment, such as a change in personnel, a new phone number, or an updated email address. Once a year, you should call each customer and review their information to ensure your files are up to date.

Pitch this exercise as a benefit. Explain to the customer that you have a policy of checking your files periodically in order to confirm their completeness and accuracy, and that you want to go over what you have on file in order to confirm that it is correct. When you are finished, ask if there's anything else you should know that would help you serve the customer better, or if there are any shipping needs you don't know about that you could help with.

Keep in mind, the shipping needs of your clients (shippers) will change often, sometimes seasonally. It's important for you to know when these changes happen, so you can easily keep up with and be prepared to handle each shipper's ever evolving needs.

Of course, with each shipment you'll need to know the destination company's name, address, contact person, and phone number. If your customers ship to the same places over and over, you'll want to keep this information on file to make it easier and faster to prepare the documentation for each load.

This information is not only necessary for your carriers (how else will they know where to take the freight if you don't tell them?), but it also gives you another potential shipper. If the consignee (the recipient of the shipment) is a manufacturer, they may have goods

aha!

Use any of the popular contact management or freight brokerage software packages to maintain your customer information. This will make the data easily accessible for anyone in the office, simple to keep current, and easy for you to monitor the status of accounts from a sales management perspective.

Many specialized software applications designed for use by freight brokers are based online. This means that you pay a monthly access fee and can access the applications and your data from any internet-connected Windows PC, Mac, or even a smartphone or tablet.

your carrier can pick up after dropping off your initial shipper's load. If the consignee has freight to send back to the initial shipper—or even someone else in the same area—and your carrier can handle this load as well, the carrier gets a very productive round trip. The trucker does not have to return empty (which means generating no revenue) or take the time and effort to find a load on its own.

Be sure to find out in advance if the shipper requires a pallet exchange, which saves carriers from having to return pallets to shippers and saves shippers from having to replace pallets all the time. It works like this: Many types of goods are loaded onto pallets, which are then loaded onto trucks. Many drivers carry empty pallets in their trucks. When they receive a load on pallets, they exchange their empty pallets for those used by the shipper for the materials just picked up. When the driver reaches the destination, the loaded pallets are swapped for empty ones, replenishing the driver's supply.

When you complete a load sheet for each shipment, include the identification numbers of the tractor and trailer that hauled the load. The carriers will provide you with their equipment numbers; it's standard procedure.

Carrier Information

Keep up-to-date information on carriers even if you don't have any loads for them at the moment. By maintaining files on carriers, you will know immediately which routes they travel and what kinds of trucks they have. This will help you select a carrier quickly when a shipper calls. Keep the following information:

- ▶ Carrier's name
- ▶ Type of carrier (contract, common, etc.)
- ▶ Physical address
- ▶ Billing address, if different from physical address
- ▶ All telephone numbers (cell phones, voice mail, fax, pagers), including any toll-free numbers
- ▶ All email addresses
- ▶ Contact person (in most cases, the dispatcher)
- ▶ Other terminals, phone numbers, and contacts
- ▶ Type and size of equipment available
- ▶ Motor carrier's license number
- ▶ Federal tax identification number
- ▶ Whether or not the carrier offers pallet exchanges

▶ Carrier's traffic lanes and backhaul requirements

Beyond the basic information about a carrier that helps you make the selection, you should obtain the following additional data before you actually give that carrier a load:

▶ Copy of current insurance certificates and updates

▶ Certificate of authority

▶ Copy of current general-commodity tariff and updates (if applicable)

There are several online-based services you can subscribe to as a freight broker to help you quickly find carriers, negotiate fees, and maintain up-to-date records. DAT Solutions, LLC's DAT RateView service (www.dat.com/products/rateview) will help you find carriers and negotiate rates based on timely and localized information.

These key documents prove that the carrier is licensed to transport freight and is insured if cargo is lost or damaged. You should not only confirm that the carrier is insured, but also note when the insurance expires. When that date arrives, check with the carrier for proof that the coverage has been renewed. Certificates of insurance usually include a provision that the holder will be notified by the company upon cancellation of coverage.

In addition to these items, ask your carriers for a statement that they assume full responsibility for paying all fuel taxes, including ton-mile taxes (taxes based on the weight and distance), in all states through which they travel. Also, while on lease or contract, they should pay fines for any and all violations incurred. Though carriers generally make it a standard part of their business operation to pay these fines, you should obtain a written agreement to that effect and place it in your files.

You should also retain any correspondence, agreements, rate quotations, policy changes, memos, etc., along with copies of all contracts, bills of lading, and invoices you send or receive.

Finding Carriers

There are tens of thousands of carriers operating in the United States. Your job as a broker is to identify the ones that provide services your customers need and to confirm their reliability before using them.

You'll find carriers listed in a number of directories, trade magazines, and online services. Word-of-mouth is also a good way to find carriers; as you're out there networking, pay attention to what others are saying about particular trucking companies and follow up on good reports.

You can also look for trucks at truck stops and on the road. When you see trucks that are clean and well-maintained, speak to the driver and find out something about the company. If it isn't practical to speak to the driver, make a note of the company name and headquarters location (it will be on the truck or the cab) and give the company a call.

"For 18 years, I've written down the names of trucking companies I see on the highway," says Bloomingdale, Illinois-based freight broker Ron Williamson. "I'll call that company and ask if it has any extra trucks it can provide us."

Of course, don't overlook the internet as a source for carriers. There are a number of online databases that allow shippers and carriers to post their freight and equipment needs. (See the Appendix for a sample listing of these resources.)

Once you've found a carrier that might be useful, you need more information before you turn a load over to it. Ask for copies of the carrier's certificate of authority, current insurance certificates, and current tariff. You should also get references from satisfied customers and take the time to check those references. Finally, check a credit reporting bureau or financial rating service to find out what the carrier's financial condition is. You want to be sure the carriers you work with are reliable and financially sound.

Avoid using major carriers that have terminals all over the country. These carriers do not take loads directly from pickup to destination; rather, they relay a load from one terminal point to another. This process takes additional time and increases the amount of handling, which increases the risk of loss or damage. It's better if the driver who picks up the load delivers it.

Some carriers use a procedure called pooling, where loads are dropped and left until a driver with the proper equipment and destination is available to pick them up. Though this may sound like an effective practice, it causes delays in transit time, and you should avoid carriers that employ this method. Such a policy will give you a competitive edge by enabling your shippers to meet tight delivery schedules.

Rates and Commissions

In the beginning, it's a good idea to handle full truckloads (FTLs), only because they're easier to deal with than less-than-truckload (LTL) shipments. It's impractical for many carriers to handle a partial load; you would need to arrange for the driver to pick up two or more LTL shipments headed for the same destination. That may seem a bit overwhelming when you're just getting started, but as you gain experience, you'll be able to handle both FTL and LTL shipments easily.

Freight charges are based on a number of variables, but the two main factors are the weight of the load and the distance it must travel. Rates are also affected by the type of truck needed, whether the driver needs to make one or more stops to pick up the freight, and whether the driver needs to make more than one stop to deliver the goods. Each shipment is entitled to one pickup and one delivery with no extra charge; you can usually negotiate the rate for additional stops with the carrier.

Before you begin shopping for rates for specific shipments, get an idea of the current "going rates" for the types of shipments you're likely to be handling. You can do this by requesting copies of tariffs from several carriers and studying them.

Many shippers—especially large companies with experienced traffic departments—will not leave it up to you to quote a rate but will tell you how much they are willing to pay. If this amount is unreasonable, you'll need to negotiate with the shipper or decline to handle the load.

Calculating freight pricing is not a simple process. Carriers negotiate rates based on commodity, value, equipment availability, volume, customer-service factors, and payment history, among other things. As a broker, you need to know what the market issues are, as well as what can cause increases or decreases in the per-mile rate, such as driver shortages, fuel surcharges, seasonal changes, toll roads, and so on.

stat fact

Annual revenue from trucking each year is around $700 billion—more than 80 percent of total revenue earned by all domestic transport modes.

Your income is generated by the commissions you earn on each load. You'll be paid one of two ways: You can bill the shipper the amount you are going to pay the carrier plus the amount of your commission, or the carrier can bill the shipper directly and then pay you a commission from its revenue.

The most common way to handle billing and commissions is to have the carrier bill you, and then you bill your customers (the shippers). Cherry Hill, New Jersey-based freight

▶ Know Your Limits

As a broker, by law you may not charge or receive compensation from a motor carrier for brokerage service if you own or have a material interest in the shipment. You are also not able to exercise control over the shipment because you own the shipper, the shipper owns your company, or there is a common ownership of the two.

In addition, you may not give or offer to give anything of value to any shipper or consignee (or their officers or employees) other than inexpensive advertising items that are distributed for promotional purposes.

broker Bill Tucker says this is much easier and less confusing for your customers than if they are billed directly by the carrier.

If the carrier bills your customer directly, your customers will receive multiple styles of bills on a variety of billing cycles, and they will have to do the extra work of matching up the bill to the shipment. "When their computer generates a bill of lading for the broker and the carrier bills them, it gets confusing," Tucker says. "Nowadays, almost all freight brokers bill the shipper and pay the carrier. It's much simpler for the shipper."

As a freight broker, your commission is negotiable. You can get whatever the traffic will bear. The average broker's commission is between 8 and 15 percent of the shipping charges, sometimes higher, and a new broker can typically expect to earn between 8 and 10 percent.

"It all comes down to negotiating," says Indianapolis-based freight broker Chuck Andrews. "If you're in a highly competitive market area—like in Atlanta, where there is a lot of freight and not very many trucks—your commission will be much lower than the industry average."

Keep in mind that your commission is your gross revenue, and out of that you must pay your overhead: rent, taxes, payroll, sales commissions, utilities, debts, etc. Williamson estimates that most brokers are lucky to earn a net profit of one to two percent after expenses.

Although you, your carriers, and your shippers need to agree on the total freight expenses for shipments, the prices of transporting freight can be broken down into smaller units. Those numbers are used to help carriers measure their own profitability and by shippers to set prices of their goods and determine profit levels. For example, carriers are interested in the total fee for any given trip, and they also want to know their fee per mile. Shippers are often interested in the cost by weight, typically measured in 100-pound units and referred to as "cost per hundredweight" (abbreviated "cwt"). These numbers are easy to calculate with simple arithmetic.

Quoting Rates

To quote a rate for a customer, follow these ten steps:

1. Find out the point of origin.
2. Find out the destination.
3. Determine the gross weight of the load.
4. Ask if the carrier will need to make stop-offs or split pickups.
5. Check whether pallets are required.
6. Find out when the load(s) will be ready for pickup.
7. Find out when the load(s) can be/need to be delivered.
8. Ask if appointments are necessary at origin or destination.
9. Find out who gets billed for the freight charges.
10. Obtain the frequency and number of similar shipments.

► Profit Prophet

When someone is considering starting a business, often one of his or her first questions is: "How soon will I start making money?" What they really mean is: "How soon will I start making a profit?" For a freight brokerage, the answer to that question is "It depends."

You'll start generating revenue with your first shipment. How long you take to actually begin making a profit will depend on the size of your operation, your monthly overhead expenses, how many customers you had when you opened your doors, and the thoroughness and aggressiveness of your business plan. Indianapolis-based freight broker Chuck Andrews says that if you have shippers lined up from the beginning and you're aggressive, you could be profitable within 90 days. But if you only have a few customers and aren't able to move a lot of freight, it could take a year or more.

With this information, you'll be able to contact carriers for quotes that will be accurate. Few things are more frustrating in this business than to quote a rate based on incomplete information. A quote will be impacted if the customer needs extra services that you have to charge for. If you didn't calculate these fees into your initial quote, then you have to tell the client that their final bill will be higher than your original estimate. Needless to say, customers don't like this, and you could lose future business as a result. Once you quote a price, your clients will expect you to adhere to it.

Documents

Once you match a load with a carrier, you must fill out a number of forms. This is something you can do manually, or utilizing specialized software can help you streamline the process.

First, you and the carrier need to enter into an agreement covering current and future dealings. The Transportation Intermediaries Association provides sample agreements in its New Broker Kit (www.tianet.org/TIAnetOrg/Meetings/Event_Display_TIACon. aspx?EventKey=NBK), but the freight brokers we talked with recommended that you develop your own contracts, agreements, and forms, customizing them to your particular operation. To do this, you'll need to consult with an attorney who specializes in this industry.

Once you have a carrier agreement on file, you need to send the carrier a load confirmation and rate agreement form for each specific load. When the carrier picks up the load from the shipper, the shipper will give the carrier a bill of lading listing the goods being transported and any special arrangements the driver needs to make for the load. When the driver reaches the consignee (recipient of the shipment), he needs to have someone there sign for the load.

If an independent contractor unloads the freight at the consignee's location, the driver needs to obtain a contract labor receipt from this worker. Depending on your arrangement with the carrier, the driver or trucking company will invoice you, the shipper, or the consignee for transportation services.

Carrier/Broker Agreement

The carrier/broker agreement outlines the terms under which you will work with a given carrier. It's designed to apply to all the dealings you have with a particular carrier and should also provide for any future changes.

When writing the carrier/broker agreement, make sure to do all of the following:

- ▶ Note the carrier's motor carrier (MC) or license number, full corporate name, and address.
- ▶ If you will be working with this carrier on a contract basis, state that the freight and rates will be negotiated for each shipment.
- ▶ State that the carrier is liable for any damage or loss to the freight that occurs while the carrier transports it.
- ▶ Note that the carrier is responsible for any personal injury or damage to vehicles or equipment that occurs while the freight is in the carrier's possession.
- ▶ State when the carrier will receive payment and what the carrier must provide before you will pay (such as bills of lading).

Figure 3–1 on page 40 shows a sample Carrier/Broker Agreement.

Load Confirmation and Rate Agreement

Once a carrier agrees to move a given load, you should complete and send a load confirmation and rate agreement form. This should include the name and address of both the shipper and the consignee, a trip number (for tracking purposes), any information on extra pickups or stops, pickup and delivery dates, a brief description of the commodity to be shipped, and your commission or brokerage fee structure. See Figure 3–2 on page 41 for a sample Load Confirmation and Rate Agreement.

Bill of Lading

At the time of the pickup, the shipper will provide the driver with a bill of lading. This form will include information on the nature and size of the load, its destination, and any required special handling. The driver signs the bill of lading as an acknowledgment of receiving the load described by the shipper.

The bill of lading is prepared and handled by the shipper and the carrier. As the broker, you will not be directly concerned with it, but you need to keep a signed copy in

Sample Carrier/Broker Agreement

This agreement is entered into between Jiffy Freight Brokers, hereinafter referred to as "Broker," and _____, hereinafter referred to as "Carrier."

Whereas Broker is a transportation broker engaged in the business of selling or negotiating transportation, and whereas Carrier is a motor carrier operating in interstate commerce.

1. The terms of the agreement shall be continuous from signing date.

2. Freight and rate shall be set and agreed upon at the time of each movement.

3. Termination of this agreement can be instituted by either party by giving thirty (30) days' notice in writing to the other party.

4. The Carrier shall be liable for all loss, damage, or liability incurred by transportation of property arranged for by the Broker while being transported by the Carrier.

5. In the event of disagreement or dispute, and if legal action is taken, the prevailing party will be entitled to legal fees.

6. Carrier will be paid within 15 days of receipt of clean bills.

7. This agreement contains the entire contract agreement and no additions can be made unless in writing or initialing by both parties.

In witness whereof, the parties hereto have signed their names on this
_____ day of _____, 20_____, in _____
_____.
        City   State

Company: Jiffy Freight Brokers   Company: _____

                1111 Baker St.   _____

                Columbus, OH 11111   _____

By: _____   By: _____

Witness: _____   Witness: _____

FIGURE 3–1: **Sample Carrier/Broker Agreement**

Sample Load Confirmation and Rate Agreement

jfB *Jiffy Freight Brokers*

Fax date: 11/12/XX

Carrier: Watson Trucking

Trip number: 5546

Carrier fax: (555) 555-5555

Driver must call JFB for dispatch. The following is for information only.

Shipper:

Bob's Frozen Dinners
Kansas City, MO
Extra Pickups:

Consignee:

Adler Refrigeration
Columbus, OH
Extra Stops:

Pickup date: 11/10/xx

I.O.# 4418

Deliver date: 11/12/xx

Commodity: Corn Dog

Comments: _____

_____

_____

Jiffy Freight Brokers charges 9% brokerage without advance and 11% with advance. If you need more than 50% of truck pay in advances, brokerage will be 15%. JFB will not advance more than 65% of truck pay.

Gross Agreed Charges: $500.00

Please refer to the TRIP NUMBER on your invoice: TRIP# 5546
All invoices must include a signed delivery receipt and be sent to:

Jiffy Freight Brokers
1111 Baker St.
Columbus, OH 11111

The undersigned hereby acknowledges as correct and accepts the referenced shipment on behalf of carrier. It is agreed that the charges indicated above are inclusive. Invoicing by the carrier and payment by Jiffy Freight Brokers creates a valid contract of carrier shipment.

Please sign this confirmation and fax to (555) 555-5556 or email to admin@jfb.com.

By: _____   By: _____

Watson Trucking   Jiffy Freight Brokers

FIGURE 3–2: **Sample Load Confirmation and Rate Agreement**

your files. The carrier usually sends this to you, along with its invoice for transportation services.

Contract Labor Receipt

Drivers may occasionally work with contract laborers who unload trucks once they reach the consignee. If they do, the laborer will give the driver a contract labor receipt, which the carrier sends to you. The driver or carrier pays the laborer and turns to you for reimbursement. If your shipper is willing to cover this cost, pay it. Even if your shipper doesn't want to pay for contract labor, you may want to consider absorbing the expense so you can maintain good relations with the driver and carrier. See Figure 3–3 for a sample Contract Labor Receipt.

Sample Contract Labor Receipt

Being the recipient of the below listed contract price, and an independent businessperson and contractor, I am fully responsible for the payment of my own taxes thereon, including self-employment taxes, income taxes, and all other applicable taxes.

I contract to load _____ unload _____ loads of _____

_____ for the amount of $_____.

Signed (Contractor) _____

Social Security or Fed ID # _____

Street address_____

City _____ State _____ Zip _____

Driver _____

Date_____

FIGURE 3–3: **Sample Contract Labor Receipt**

Invoices

After making the delivery and obtaining proof of delivery, the carrier sends you an invoice, along with the bill of lading. With these documents, you can prepare your own invoice to send to the shipper. (Unless, of course, the carrier bills the shipper directly.)

stat fact

According to the American Trucking Association, motor carriers collect 87 percent of total revenue earned by all modes of transportation.

Your invoice should include the billing date, the dates of pickup and delivery, the origin and destination, what was shipped (commodity, pieces and total weight), and additional fees (such as fees for exceeding weight limits or charges for contract labor). Bill your shipper as soon as you receive the complete invoice and bill of lading from your carrier.

If the shipper is sending the delivery "collect," then you bill the consignee rather than the shipper. The shipper should provide you with billing information on these shipments. See Figure 3–4, page 44, for a sample invoice.

Contract of Carriage

A contract of carriage is not a document itself, but it's important that you understand the concept and what it includes. Many otherwise well-informed transportation professionals view the bill of lading as a contract of carriage—a common misconception. "A bill of lading is certainly a receipt used in a contract of carriage, but there are many elements required by that contract that are generally not stated on the bill of lading," explained Bill Tucker. "Some examples: the price agreed to in the contract, all the services to be provided, rules to be used to handle exceptions, and accessorial charges that may be applicable."

What makes up a contract of carriage? "A contract of carriage between a common carrier and a shipper (with or without a broker being involved) usually consists of some form of bill of lading, whether 'standard' or not, plus all the tariff provisions, pricing, rules, and service descriptions," Tucker says. "Also part of the total contract is the intent of the parties; the regulatory rules that must be followed, whether federal, state or local; and all the other 'usage of trade' and precedent within which this transaction has occurred."

Are You on a Mission?

At any given moment, most business owners have a very clear understanding of the mission of their companies. They know what they are doing, how, and where it's being done, and

Sample Invoice

 **Jiffy Freight Brokers**

1111 Baker Street
Columbus, OH 11111

Invoice: 005546   Date: 11/12/XX

Bill to:

P/U: 11/10/xx   Del: 11/12/XX

Bob's Frozen Dinners
2222 E. Havisham Rd.
Kansas City, MO 00000

Carr: WATTRU   Trip# 005546

P/O: 4481   B/L:

Shipper:

Bob's Frozen Dinners
BOBFRO 2222 E. Havisham Rd.
Kansas City, MO 00000

Consignee:

Adler Refrigeration
ADREF 3333 Cratchett Ln.
Columbus, OH 00000

Pieces	Description	Identifier	Weight	Rate	Charges
	Corn Dogs	PE			$700.00
	Unloading				45.00
	Invoice Total				$745.00

This account is due and payable in 7 days.

FIGURE 3–4: **Sample Invoice**

who their customers are. Problems can arise, however, when that mission is not clearly articulated into a statement, written down, and communicated to others.

Even in a very small company, a written mission statement helps everyone involved see the big picture and keeps them focused on the true goals of the business. At a minimum, your mission statement should define who your primary customers are, identify the services you provide, and describe the geographical location in which you operate. A mission statement should be short—usually just one sentence and certainly no more than three. A good idea is to cap it at 100 words. Anything longer than that isn't a mission statement and will probably confuse your employees. Your mission statement doesn't have to be clever or catchy—just accurate.

To develop an effective mission statement, ask yourself these questions:

▶ Why does my company exist? Whom do we serve? What is our purpose?

▶ What are our strengths, weaknesses, opportunities, and threats?

▶ Considering the above, along with our expertise and resources, what business should we be in?

▶ What is important to us? What do we stand for?

Smyrna, Tennessee-based MCD Transportation's mission statement reads: "To provide our customers with dependable transportation services based on fair and competitive pricing programs with an emphasis on customer service for all concerned parties. To be receptive to customers' needs and react in a professional and timely manner. To recognize customers, carriers and vendors as our only assets for continued success." Not only is the mission statement used as a marketing tool, but employees are also encouraged to periodically review it and suggest any changes they think are needed.

Use the Mission Statement Worksheet in Figure 3–5, page 46, to help you write one for your business.

For help creating a full business plan that includes a mission statement, consider using one of the following standalone software or online computer applications:

▶ BizPlanBuilder—www.businesspowertools.com/project/bizplanbuilder-small-cloud-business-plan-software-app-template-crowd-fund

▶ Business Plan Pro—www.businessplanpro.com

▶ LivePlan—www.liveplan.com

▶ Plan Write—www.brs-inc.com/pwb.asp

Mission Statement Worksheet

To develop an effective mission statement, ask yourself these four questions:

1. Why does my company exist? Whom do we serve? What is our purpose? _____

   _____

   _____

   _____

2. What are our strengths, weaknesses, opportunities, and threats? _____

   _____

   _____

   _____

3. Considering the above, along with our expertise and resources, what business should we be in? _____

   _____

   _____

   _____

4. What is important to us? What do we stand for? _____

   _____

   _____

   _____

Now that you've answered those questions, you are ready to write your own mission statement. Use the area below.

_____

_____

_____

_____

FIGURE 3–5: **Mission Statement Worksheet**

Seasonal Issues

It's likely that no industry is more affected by seasonal issues than transportation. The volume and type of freight moving often depends on the time of year. At times, there will be an abundance of trucks and drivers eager to haul loads, and other times balancing the federal budget will look like a simpler task than finding a single truck and driver. For example, even though you may not handle produce, produce season can cause a lack of trucks that affects your ability to serve your customers. Another busy season is, of course, the fourth quarter, as holiday merchandise and year-end orders are moving.

In addition to equipment availability, there's also the issue of weather. Snow and ice can create dangerous driving conditions and affect transit times. Fog and rain can be year-round problems in various parts of the country. In dry seasons, areas prone to wildfires may experience road closures due to heavy smoke and fire jumping across highways. Tornadoes usually last just a few minutes and hurricanes take less than a day to pass through an area, but the damage they leave behind can have a major impact on the ability of truckers to move cargo.

Beyond the mechanics of seasonal issues—getting the freight on trucks and moved—is the impact of seasons on your revenue. If possible, build your customer base with accounts that are not strongly seasonal in nature. Expect some slowdowns at certain times of the year; prepare for those periods and use the time to evaluate your business and deal with any internal issues that need attention. You can also increase your sales efforts during slow periods. It's very important to understand your customer base so you can accurately predict and prepare for the slow periods, especially when it comes to adjusting for a drop in cash flow.

The Impact of 9/11 on Brokers

The terrorist attacks of 9/11 have prompted increased security measures for all modes of transportation. An issue of particular impact on brokers has to do with who is driving the trucks. "You used to be able to drive right up to the shipping dock, get your load, and go," says Joe Workman, president of Transportation Resources, Inc., a freight management company with headquarters in Winter Park, Florida. "Now, in many cases, drivers have to show identification before they are admitted to the premises, and some companies require drivers to be pre-qualified before picking up a load. Shippers are more concerned than they've ever been about who is hauling their freight."

Workman says many shippers want to be able to maintain communication with drivers by either cell phone or satellite. "If drivers don't have reliable on-the-road communication means, we can't use them, and that cuts back on our available trucks."

If you want to handle air freight, you should know that airlines now require cargo to come from known shippers. "Somebody with the carrier has to know you and vouch for you," says Workman. "It's harder now for new people to do business."

Customers who ship sensitive or hazardous materials have special requirements, and you should find out what those are as far in advance as possible. Workman advises, "Know your customers—know who they are, what they do, and what you're picking up."

4

What Can
Go Wrong?

I n the freight business, the ability to deal with problems

is essential. What can go wrong? Everything! No matter

how well you handle your part of the process, there are

certain things that are out of your control, but for which

your shippers will look to you for assistance and solutions.

Because brokers are not carriers, they are generally

not liable for loss or damage of a shipment while being

transported. They can, however, be held liable if they are negligent, or if they offer services other than brokerage. Aside from the liability issue, part of your service package should include assisting your customers with problems whether you are responsible or not.

Transit Delays

It's virtually impossible to list all the reasons freight might be delayed in transit. Weather is always a major concern. Trucks break down, traffic gets heavy, highways are closed, drivers get sick—and your customers will expect you to deal with it all. Cathy Davis of MCD Transportation in Smyrna, Tennessee, recalled a nightmare of a situation involving the proverbial "driver from hell." She said, "The freight was held hostage [for payment] by an owner/operator even though the company had signed a contract agreeing to the terms. We had to pay air freight charges to ship more material to keep the customer's production line going."

Most of your problems won't be that dramatic, but any time the freight does not move precisely as expected, your customers will be looking to you for situation management and information.

Cargo Loss or Damage Claims

As the broker, you are not responsible for cargo loss or damage claims. Keep in mind that although common carriers are generally liable for loss or damage to the goods they carry, they are not responsible for losses occurring due to acts of God, war, or government; through defaults on the part of the shipper; or for losses resulting from the nature of the goods.

Whatever the reason for the loss or damage, you need to understand the process of dealing with claims and be prepared to assist your shippers when necessary. If the driver does not review the bill of lading and inspect the freight before the shipment is loaded, the carrier doesn't really have any options other than to pay a claim if the cargo is damaged or short when it arrives at the destination.

warning

Sometimes employees of the shipper or consignee, or at the warehouses those companies use, try to cover damages and shortages they cause by trying to make it look like the carrier's fault. Protect yourself and your carriers while maintaining your relationship with customers and warehouses by insisting that drivers do their jobs thoroughly, which means checking the load and making complete documentation.

There will be times when the loading crew makes mistakes but realizes them after the fact and initiates a bill of lading change, which relieves the driver and carrier of potential claim responsibility. But you cannot rely on them to do so, and drivers should examine each load to be sure the documents match the shipment and sign for exactly what is received.

There will be times when it's impractical or impossible for the driver to thoroughly inspect a shipment. For example, if the carrier drops a trailer at the shipper's location to be loaded by the shipper's employees and then picked up later for transport, the driver won't know what went on the trailer. Or if the shipper assembles and shrink-wraps pallets of boxes, the driver may not be able to precisely count the number of boxes on each pallet. In those cases, the driver should write "shipper's load and count" and/or "contents and condition unknown" on the bill of lading, which shifts the responsibility for shortages, overages, and concealed damage back to the shipper.

tip

If a particular driver or carrier repeatedly incurs damage claims, especially if they are filed by different shippers, find out why. The drivers may be doing a sloppy job of securing the freight or they may be stealing some of the goods they haul. You need to identify and correct the problem at its source or stop using that driver or carrier.

At the destination, the consignee's receiving person should also inspect and count the shipment and note any discrepancies or visible damage on the delivery receipt.

When you learn of a potential claim—possibly from the shipper, consignee, or driver—immediately notify the carrier and dispatcher. Sometimes they hear of a possible problem from the driver making the delivery and let you know. Or you might not find out about a claim until you receive the proof of delivery and bill of lading with damage notations.

Not every damage notation results in a claim. For example, it's possible for the contents to be fine even though the exterior of a box was damaged.

How the claim is handled often depends on the amount in question and the history and reputation of the shipper. For a small claim where damage was clearly noted on the delivery receipt, the carrier will probably pay without a detailed investigation. For a larger claim, the carrier may send out an inspector to take a look at the damaged goods. A carrier can decline to pay a claim if it determines that the cause of the damage was inadequate packaging, so consignees should keep the damaged items and the packing materials until the claim is resolved.

Shippers usually have standard forms used to file their claims. All you need to do is provide the shipper with the name and address of the carrier in question and, if necessary, assist them in reaching a fair and prompt settlement.

If your shipper is not familiar with procedures for filing a claim, explain that he or she will need to submit the following information to the carrier on a signed form:

- ▶ Carrier's name and address
- ▶ Total claim amount
- ▶ Date of pickup
- ▶ Date of delivery
- ▶ Claim history
- ▶ Shipper's full name and address
- ▶ Consignee's full name and address
- ▶ Damages or shortages

The shipper will also need to attach any required or appropriate supporting documentation, including:

- ▶ Freight bill
- ▶ Bill of lading
- ▶ Invoice
- ▶ Inspection report, if any
- ▶ Itemized statement of loss

The carrier has 30 days to either pay the claim or acknowledge the claim and advise the shipper what else it needs to process the claim. Federal law requires carriers to investigate claims promptly and either settle the claim within 120 days or advise the claimant of any delay and then continue advising the claimant of the status of the claim every 60 days.

Responding to Problems

It's possible for you to lose a customer over a service problem that wasn't technically your fault. In most cases, though, you'll find that shippers understand when things go wrong—when drivers do not show up, when equipment breaks down, when crashes occur on the highway, and so on.

What's critical is that you don't ignore problems or try to hide them from your shippers or carriers. Be proactive. When you find out about a problem, make sure everyone who needs to know is notified immediately, and then do everything you can to get the freight back on the road.

Locating and Setting Up

One of the most appealing aspects of a freight brokerage is that your physical startup requirements are relatively small. Unlike a carrier or freight forwarder, you don't need a warehouse or loading dock, nor do you need to invest in a fleet of trucks. Your customers aren't likely to come to your location, so you don't need to worry about an impressive reception area or elegant offices.

While there are some definite advantages to a commercial location, a freight brokerage is an ideal business to start and run from home.

Cathy Davis started MCD Transportation from home, but the company grew enough to move into commercial space after just eight months. Chuck Andrews works from a commercial location in Indianapolis, but has agents around the country who work out of their homes. Where you operate depends on your resources and goals for your company. Many brokers start from home with the goal of moving into a commercial office space as soon as they are established with a few clients, and this is an excellent strategy.

stat fact

More than 70 percent of all communities in the United States receive all their products and goods by motor carrier.

The major benefit of starting a homebased business is the fact that it significantly reduces the amount of startup and initial operating capital you'll need. There are also some tax advantages, based on the amount of physical space within your home you dedicate to being your office. Be sure to consult with your accountant about this as you prepare your annual tax returns for yourself and your business.

There's a lot more to consider than simply the upfront cash requirement. Do you have a separate room within your home for an office, or will you have to work at the dining room table? Can you set up a comfortable workstation with all the tools and equipment you will need? Can you separate your work area from the rest of the house so you can have privacy when you are working—and get away from "the office" when you're not?

▶ Working from Home Requires Adjustment

One of the biggest challenges of working from home, especially if you've never done this before, is time management. You need to learn how to avoid distractions and focus on work during your work day, as opposed to taking frequent breaks to do things around the house, like watching television, cleaning, gardening, doing laundry, or playing with your dog. This requires discipline.

You'll also need to adjust to the lack of in-person social interaction with coworkers and clients. Your main communication with other people will be via email and telephone. You can't simply walk to the next cubicle or office and strike up a conversation with a coworker when working from home. If you've worked in a traditional office environment, the lack of in-person social interaction that results in working from home will require some getting used to.

If you're planning to hire administrative help, your office needs to be large enough to provide them with adequate workspace, and you need available parking. Plus, there are additional insurance requirements associated with having employees work from your home.

tip

To learn more about shared office space options in your community using any internet search engine, enter the search phrase, "shared office space," followed by a comma, and then add your city and state. For example, type "shared office space, Boston, Massachusetts."

By contrast, starting in a commercial location requires more initial cash than starting from home. If you decide on this, your range of options is fairly broad, and your choice should be guided largely by the goals you've set for your business in terms of market and growth. Consider office buildings, light-industrial parks, and executive suites.

In many cities and communities, there are also fully furnished, shared office suites that can be rented on a month-to-month basis from companies like Regus (www.regus.com) that include a receptionist, shared conference room(s), and private offices. One benefit to this option is that there's no long-term lease to sign, but the monthly fee will be slightly higher than a traditional commercial office space.

Unless you have an extremely large home, you'll find that a commercial location allows you to create a setup that is more efficient than what you might be able to do in a spare bedroom or home office. Just be careful when shopping for a space. Rental rates and leasing terms vary, so make sure you comparison shop.

Put It All in Writing

Whether your goal is a solo homebased operation, a small family business, or a transportation empire, you will need to start with a written business plan. This helps you think through what you're doing, see your strengths and weaknesses, and figure out ways to overcome challenges on paper before you have to face them in real life. Writing a business plan is not just a necessary chore; it creates the foundation and sets the vision for your company.

Your business plan should include worst-case scenarios. You'll benefit from thinking ahead about what you'll do if things don't go as you want them to. Think about things such as equipment breakdowns, employees who don't show up (even for valid reasons), uncollectible invoices, and other challenges that are part of doing business today.

The Agent Option

Some brokers may opt to use agents to develop a wider scope of operations. In this context, agents are independent contractors who represent your company in a given area. This enables you to offer a local presence when you may not have the volume to justify opening your own office.

Along these lines, you may want to consider starting out as an agent rather than a broker. Chuck Andrews's brokerage company is based in Indianapolis, but he has agents in Texas, Florida, Georgia, West Virginia, and Indiana. Because his agents are not running independent brokerage companies, and because they are homebased, their startup materials are minimal and typically consist of an internet-connected computer, printer, telephone, fax machine, and some file cabinets. The agent's work is very similar to what a broker does, but the agent functions under auspices of the broker and the broker is responsible for issues, such as paying carriers and maintaining the required surety bonds.

Again, if you opt to start off as an agent working for another company, as opposed to launching your own freight brokerage business, the initial financial responsibilities are much lower, and you can begin gaining real-world experience almost immediately. If you opt to pursue this approach, consider participating in a freight brokerage training program and then applying for an agent job with established brokers.

Naming Your Company

Your company name is an important marketing tool. A well-chosen name works very hard for you; choosing an ineffective name means you have to work much harder at marketing your company and letting people know what you have to offer.

tip

Anytime you register a company domain name, always choose the dot-com (.com) extension. While hundreds of other domain name extensions are available, and you can register some of those as well, most people are accustomed to typing dot-com after a website address they want to visit and will do this automatically. If your domain name ends with .info, .net, or .co, for example, you could wind up losing business.

Plan on spending less than $25 per year for each domain name you register. You'll then most likely need to pay to have your company website created and hosted on your behalf. In today's business world, having a company website, in addition to a presence on social media (particularly Facebook and LinkedIn), is essential.

Your company name should clearly identify what you do in a way that appeals to your target market. It should be short, catchy, and memorable. It should also be easy to pronounce and spell—people who can't say your company name may use you, but they won't refer anyone else to you.

When choosing a company name, also make sure the website domain name for it is available. To do this, go to any internet domain name registrar, such as GoDaddy. com (www.godaddy.com), and within the Find Your Perfect Domain Name field that's displayed on the main page, enter your desired company name. If it's available, register that domain name.

Cathy Davis gave serious thought to several names before deciding to use her initials. Chuck Andrews chose his company's name—Midwest Freight Brokers, Inc.—based on its location and the service the company provides. "We're located in the Midwest, freight is what we do, and brokers are what we are," he says. Ron Williamson used a combination of his and his wife's initials to come up with RJW Logistics, Inc., because he wanted a name no one else was using.

Take a systematic approach to naming your company. For descriptive purposes, incorporate the words "Freight Brokers," "Freight Broker," or "Logistics" into the name whenever possible. Once you've decided on two or three possibilities, take the following steps:

▶ *Check the name for effectiveness and functionality.* Does it quickly and easily convey what you do? Is it easy to say and spell? Is it memorable in a positive way? Ask several of your friends and associates to serve as a focus group to help you evaluate the company name's impact.

▶ *Search for potential conflicts in your local market.* Find out if any other local or regional business serving your market area has a similar name that might confuse the public.

▶ *Check for legal availability.* Exactly how you do this depends on the legal structure you choose. Typically, sole proprietorships and partnerships operating under a name other than that of the

aha!

When naming your company, consider creating a word that doesn't exist. This is what companies like Exxon, and Kodak did. Just be sure the syllables blend to make an ear-appealing sound, and that the name is simple enough for people to remember. Also, make sure you haven't inadvertently come up with a name that means something negative in another language, or that infringes on someone else's copyright or trademark.

owner(s) are required by the county, city, or state to register their fictitious name. Even if it's not required, it's a good idea because that means no one else can use that name. Sometimes it's as simple as filing for a "doing business as" (dba). Corporations usually operate under their corporate names. In either case, you need to check with the appropriate regulatory agency to be sure the name you choose is available.

▶ *Check for use on the internet.* If someone else is already using your name as an address on the internet, consider coming up with something else. Even if you come up with a different name for your website or use a different extension (such as .net, .co, or any of the other extensions available), the use of your name by another company could become confusing to your customers or result in lost business.

▶ *Make sure you can establish social media accounts on Facebook, LinkedIn, Twitter, and other popular services, using your chosen company name.* When it comes to having an online presence, between your website, company email addresses, and social media presence, continuity is essential.

▶ *Check to see if the name conflicts with any name listed on your state's trademark register.* Your state Department of Commerce can help you or direct you to the correct agency. You should also check with the trademark register maintained by the U.S. Patent and Trademark Office (PTO). Once the name you've chosen passes these tests, you need to protect it by registering it with the appropriate state agency; again, your state Department of Commerce can help you. If you expect to be doing business on a national level, you should also register the name with the PTO.

▶ How to Establish Yourself on Social Media

To create a free Facebook page for your business, start by visiting www.facebook.com/pages/create. To create a Twitter for Business account, visit: https://business.twitter.com, and to establish a presence on LinkedIn, visit www.linkedin.com.

In the process of creating your online presence on each social networking service, be sure to brand it with your logo and related content, and ensure that all of your contact information is prominently displayed. Use your company name as your username or Facebook page name, for example.

Brand Your Business

Once you have selected a company name, hire a graphic artist to develop a unique and eye-catching logo for your business. This will cost anywhere from $50.00 to several hundred dollars. Showcasing a professional-looking logo on your letterhead, website, business cards, invoices, within your social media presence, and within your emails, for example, will enhance your company's image and help you build credibility faster.

To have a logo created, seek out a local, freelance graphic artist or use an online service like UpWork (www.upwork.com), Freelancer (www.freelancer.com), or Fiverr (www.fiverr.com) to seek out a graphic artist who specializes in company logo design.

Be sure to describe to the graphic artist what your company does, who your target audience is, and what image you're trying to convey, in order to provide some initial creative direction. Then, make sure the graphic artist you hire signs a release giving you full legal ownership over the logo design. Follow this up by filing for a copyright and/or trademark of the logo.

To learn more about filing a copyright, visit www.copyright.gov/registration/. Filing a graphic-based trademark is a little more complicated, but it's a process you can do yourself or by hiring an attorney. To learn more, start by visiting the United States Patent and Trademark Office website (www.uspto.gov). LegalZoom (www.legalzoom.com) offers a fee-based online service to help with the copyright and trademark filing processes.

Choosing a Legal Structure

One of the first decisions you'll need to make about your freight brokerage is the legal structure of your company. This is an important decision. It affects your financial liability, the amount of taxes you pay, and the degree of ultimate control you have over the company. It also affects your ability to attract investors and ultimately sell the business. However, legal structure shouldn't be confused with operating structure. Attorney Robert S. Bernstein, managing partner with Pittsburgh-based Bernstein-Burkley PC, explains the difference: "The legal structure is the ownership structure—who actually owns the company. The operating structure defines who makes management decisions and runs the company."

Consult with both an attorney and accountant to help you choose the most ideal type of legal business structure for your freight brokerage business prior to you formally

▶ Quittin' Time?

Successful freight brokers recommend that you get practical industry experience by working for another broker, carrier, or shipper before starting your own enterprise. If you follow this advice, when do you tell your boss about your plans?

There's no one-size-fits-all answer. You need to determine where you stand ethically, legally, and practically. Take any employment-related contracts you have signed—including non-compete and confidentiality agreements—along with your employee handbook—to an attorney. This is especially important if your brokerage will either compete with or use information (such as customer lists) you obtained from your current employer.

A lawyer can review those documents, let you know whether or not you are violating the agreements, and help you understand what potential litigation you may face. Keep in mind that you can be fired for starting your own business. Most states are at-will employment states, which means you can be terminated for any reason or no reason, as long as there is no discrimination involved.

What about trying to start something on the side and building it as long as you can while still working full time? The risk you're taking there, says Cherry Hill, New Jersey-based freight broker Bill Tucker, is the image you're projecting to your customers. If you're sneaking around behind your employer's back and violating your employment contract, you're sending a message of questionable judgment and ethics to your customers and associates. This can quickly tarnish your professional reputation moving forward.

Especially if you're working for another broker as an independent agent, it's entirely possible that your employer will support your venture. Also, if, for example, you are a sales rep for a carrier, you can present your brokerage business as an opportunity for your employer. You'll still be out there drumming up business for the carrier, and other carriers as well, but you'll be doing it on a commission basis, which means the carrier will no longer have to pay the expenses associated with having you as an employee. "You can sell the partnership idea to the owner of a trucking company," Tucker says. "I know that's been done a lot of times. More and more, creative relationships are open for consideration."

establishing the business. It's important that from a legal and tax standpoint, you set up everything correctly right from the start. The decisions you make should be based on a variety of factors, including where you'll be doing business from.

A sole proprietorship is owned by the proprietor, a partnership is owned by the partners, and a corporation is owned by the shareholders. Another business structure, the limited liability company (LLC), combines the tax advantages of a sole proprietorship with the liability protection of a corporation. The rules on LLCs vary by state; check with your state's Department of Corporations for the latest requirements.

Sole proprietorships and partnerships can be operated however the owners choose. In a corporation, the shareholders typically elect directors who, in turn, elect officers who then employ other people to run and work in the company. But it's entirely possible for a corporation to have only one shareholder and to essentially function as a sole proprietorship. In any case, how you plan to operate the company should not be a major factor in your choice of legal structures.

So what goes into choosing a legal structure? The first point, says Bernstein, is who is actually making the decision on the legal structure. If you're starting the company by yourself, you don't need to take anyone else's preferences into consideration. "But if there are multiple people involved, you need to consider how you're going to relate to each other in the business," he says. "You also need to consider the issue of asset protection and limiting your liability in the event things don't go well."

Something else to think about is your target customers and what their perception will be of your structure. Bernstein says, "There is a tendency to believe that the legal form of a business has some relationship to the sophistication of the owners, with the sole proprietor as the least and the corporation as the most sophisticated." Because your target market is going to be other businesses large enough to be shipping substantial amounts of cargo, it will probably enhance your image if you incorporate.

Your image notwithstanding, the biggest advantage of forming a corporation is in the area of asset protection, which, Bernstein says, is the process of making sure that the assets you don't want to put into the business don't stand liable for business debt. However, to take advantage of the protection a corporation offers, you must respect the corporation's identity. That means maintaining the corporation as a separate entity; keeping your corporate and personal funds separate even if you are the sole shareholder; and following your state's rules regarding holding annual meetings and other record-keeping requirements.

Davis incorporated based on the advice of both her accountant and attorney; the C corporation suited her operation best for both tax and liability purposes. Andrews is incorporated, but he personally owns 100 percent of the stock, so he can essentially function with the autonomy of a sole proprietor.

You don't need an attorney to set up a corporation, LLC, or partnership, but consulting with an attorney and an accountant prior to setting up your business' legal entity is a sound business practice. Bernstein says there are plenty of good do-it-yourself books and kits on the market, and most of the state agencies that oversee corporations have guidelines you can use. LegalZoom (www.legalzoom.com) is an example of a fee-based online service that walks you through the process of setting up a corporation without an attorney.

However, it's always a good idea to have a lawyer at least look over your documents before you file them, just to make sure they are complete and will allow you to truly function as you want.

Finally, remember that your choice of legal structure is not an irrevocable decision, although if you're going to make a switch, it's easier to go from the simpler forms to the more sophisticated ones than vice versa. Bernstein says the typical pattern is to start as a sole proprietor and then move up to a corporation as the business grows. But if you need the asset protection of a corporation from the beginning, start out that way. Says Bernstein, "If you're going to the trouble of starting a business, decide on a structure and put it all together; it's worth the extra effort to make sure it's really going to work."

Insurance

Because you never actually take possession of your customers' goods, you don't need to worry about insuring them. It is carriers' responsibility to provide coverage for the value of the freight they are hauling. Generally, a certain amount of value (which may vary by carrier) is calculated into the basic freight rate, and if the actual value of the goods exceeds what the basic rate covers, the shipper can purchase additional protection from the trucking company.

Even though you don't need to worry about insuring freight, your company still has insurance issues to address. If you're homebased, do not assume your homeowner's or renter's policy covers your business equipment; chances are, it doesn't. If you're located in a commercial facility, be prepared for your landlord to require proof of certain

aha!

Sit down with your insurance agent every year and review your insurance needs, which are sure to change as your company grows. Also, insurance companies are always developing new products to meet the needs of the growing small-business market, and it's possible one of these new policies will be more appropriate for you.

levels of liability insurance when you sign the lease. In either case, you need coverage for your equipment and supplies, and workers' compensation if you have employees. You also need additional insurance coverage if you plan to have employees working from your home.

A smart approach to insurance is to find an agent who works with other freight brokers and transportation companies. The agent should be willing to help you analyze your needs, evaluate what risks you're willing to accept and what risks you need to insure against, and work with you to keep your insurance costs down.

Typically, homebased freight brokers want to make sure their equipment and supplies are covered against theft and damage by an act of God, such as fire or flood, and that they have some liability protection if someone (a customer, supplier, or employee) is injured on their property. In most cases, one of the insurance products designed for homebased businesses will provide sufficient coverage. Also, you will probably use your vehicle for business purposes, so make sure it is adequately covered.

If you opt for a commercial location, you'll need to meet the landlord's requirements for general liability coverage. You'll also want to cover your supplies, equipment, and fixtures. Once your business is up and running, consider business interruption insurance to replace lost revenue and cover related costs if you are ever unable to operate due to covered circumstances.

> **tip**
>
> When you purchase insurance on your equipment and fixtures, ask what documentation the insurance company requires before you have to file a claim. That way, you'll be sure to maintain appropriate records, and the claims process will be easier.
>
> Within your records, keep receipts for all computer equipment and related technology you purchase. Make sure you have, in writing, the computer's system configuration and serial number, for example. This also applies to other equipment, like printers, fax machines, and office telephone systems.

You may also want to carry contingency cargo insurance. This is coverage that would take over on cargo if the carrier's insurance did not fully cover the value of a load that was damaged or destroyed.

Professional Advisors

As a business owner, you may be the boss, but you can't be expected to know everything. You will occasionally need to turn to professionals for information and assistance. It's a good idea to establish a relationship with these professionals before you get into a crisis situation.

To shop for a professional service provider, ask friends and associates for recommendations. You might also check with your local chamber of commerce or trade association for referrals. Find someone who understands transportation in general and the brokerage side of it specifically, and appears eager to work with you. Check them out with the Better Business Bureau and the appropriate state licensing agency before committing yourself.

The professional service providers you are likely to need include:

tip

In addition to operating his own freight brokerage business and Brooke Transportation Training Solutions (a training program for freight brokers), Jeff Roach, his wife and business partner, and other leaders within his company also do consulting work with other freight brokers. For more information, visit www.brooketraining.com.

▶ *Attorney.* You need a lawyer who understands and practices in the area of business and transportation law, who is honest, and who appreciates your patronage. In most parts of the United States, there are many lawyers willing to compete fiercely for the privilege of serving you. Interview several, and choose one you feel comfortable with. Be sure to clarify the fee schedule ahead of time and get your agreement in writing. Keep in mind that good commercial lawyers don't come cheap; if you want good advice, you must be willing to pay for it. Your attorney should review all contracts, leases, letters of intent, and other legal documents before you sign them. They can also help you with collecting bad debts, and establishing personnel policies and procedures. Of course, if you are unsure of the legal ramifications of any situation, call your attorney immediately.

▶ *Accountant.* Among your outside advisors, your accountant is likely to have the greatest impact on the success or failure of your business. If you are forming a corporation, your accountant should counsel you on tax issues during startup. On an ongoing basis, your accountant can help you organize the statistical data concerning your business, assist in charting future actions based on past performance, and advise you on your overall financial strategy regarding purchasing, capital investment, and other matters related to your business goals. A good accountant also serves as a tax advisor, not only making sure you are in compliance with all applicable regulations, but also that you don't overpay any taxes.

During the startup phase of your business, an accountant will help you set up your internal bookkeeping operation to ensure everything is set up correctly, whether you're using general accounting/bookkeeping software, such as Intuit's QuickBooks, or specialized software for freight brokers from a company like DAT Solutions, LLC.

▶ *Insurance Agent.* A good independent insurance agent can assist you with all aspects of your business insurance, from general liability to employee benefits, and probably even handle your personal lines as well. Look for an agent who works with a wide range of insurers and understands your particular business. This agent should be willing to explain the details of various types of coverage, to consult with you to determine the most appropriate coverage, to help you understand the degree of risk you are taking, to work with you to develop risk-reduction programs, and to assist in expediting any claims.

▶ *Banker(s).* You need a business bank account and a relationship with at least one banker. Don't just choose the bank you've always done your personal banking with; it may not be the best bank for your business. Interview several bankers before deciding where to place your business. Once your account is open, maintain a relationship with the banker. Periodically sit down and review your accounts and the services you use to make sure you have the most appropriate package for your situation.

▶ *Consultants.* The consulting industry is booming—and for good reason. Consultants can provide valuable, objective input on all aspects of your business. (Keep in mind that, as a broker, you will occasionally put on a consultant's hat as you work with your customers.) Consider hiring a business consultant to evaluate your business plan, or a marketing consultant to assist you in that area. When you're ready to hire employees, a human resources consultant may help you avoid some costly mistakes. Many freight brokerages are family businesses, so it might help to consult with an expert in the areas of both family dynamics in business and succession planning. For example, after the death of her mother, Cathy Davis, Donna J. Wood took over as president (she had served as vice president), and her sister, Dionne R. Kegley, became vice president of the Smyrna, Tennessee, company. Davis had worked diligently to create a succession plan that provided a smooth transition when it became necessary. Consulting fees vary widely, depending on the individual's experience, location, and field of expertise. If you can't afford to hire a consultant, consider contacting the business school at the nearest college or university and hiring an MBA student to help you.

▶ *Computer Expert.* Your computer is your most valuable physical asset, so if you don't know much about computers, find someone to help you select a system and the appropriate software—someone who will be available to help you maintain, troubleshoot, and expand your system as you need it. Keep in mind that many of the specialized computer applications designed for freight brokers, such as those from DAT Solutions, LLC, are based online, and include interactive training and tutorials to help you learn how to use the applications. While little or no software gets installed on your computer(s), continuous and high-speed internet access is required to utilize the applications from your Windows PC or Mac computer(s).

In addition to your "live" professional advisors, you'll need a collection of resource and reference materials. The freight broker business is full of details so numerous that you can't possibly expect to remember them all. You will need broker and carrier directories, a mileage guide, and business directories. A listing of publications appears in the Appendix.

Create Your Own Advisory Board

Not even the President of the United States is expected to know everything. That's why the President surrounds himself with advisors—experts in particular areas who provide knowledge and information to help him make decisions. Savvy small-business owners in all industries use a similar strategy.

You can assemble a team of volunteer advisors to meet with you periodically to offer advice and direction. Because this isn't an official or legal entity, you have a great deal of latitude in how you set it up. Advisory boards can be structured to help with the direct operation of your company and to keep you informed on various business, legal, and financial trends that may affect you. Use these tips to set up your advisory board:

▶ *Structure a board that meets your needs.* Generally, you'll want a legal advisor, an accountant, a marketing expert, a human resources person, and perhaps a financial advisor. You may also want successful entrepreneurs from other industries who understand the basics of business and will view your operation with a fresh eye.

▶ *Ask the most successful people you can find, even if you don't know them well.* You'll be surprised at how willing people are to help another business succeed.

▶ *Be clear about what you are trying to do.* Let your prospective advisors know what your goals are and that you don't expect them to take on an active management role or to assume any liability for your company or for the advice they offer.

▶ *Don't worry about compensation.* Advisory board members are rarely compensated with more than lunch or dinner. Of course, if a member of your board provides a direct service—for example, if an attorney reviews a contract or an accountant prepares a financial statement—then they should be paid at their normal rate. But that's not part of their job as an advisory board member. Keep in mind that even though you don't write them a check, your advisory board members will likely benefit in a variety of tangible and nontangible ways. Being on your board will expose them to ideas and perspectives they may not otherwise see and will also expand their own network.

▶ Choose Equipment That's Reliable

Although multifunction devices—such as a copier/printer/fax machine or a fax/telephone/answering machine—may cost less initially and take up less space in your office than stand-alone items, you'll lose all of these functions simultaneously if the equipment fails. Also, consider the machine's efficiency rating and cost to operate; compare that with stand-alone items before buying. However, these machines are more reliable than ever, so one could be right for you.

There are a variety of professional voicemail services you can subscribe to as a small business that offer key features that will enhance the professional image of your company. However, try to avoid using complex voicemail systems that make it difficult for people to ultimately leave a message or reach you, especially when a time-sensitive situation arises.

Many voicemail services will automatically transcribe incoming phone messages into a text and then send you an email or text message with the transcript of each incoming message.

▶ *Consider the group dynamics when holding meetings.* You may want to meet with all the members together or in small groups of one or two. It all depends on how they relate to each other and what you need to accomplish.

▶ *Ask for honesty, and don't be offended when you get it.* Your pride might be hurt when someone points out something you're doing wrong, but the awareness will be beneficial in the long run.

▶ *Learn from failure as well as success.* Encourage board members to tell you about their mistakes so you can avoid making them.

▶ *Respect the contribution your board members are making.* Let them know you appreciate how busy they are, and don't abuse or waste their time.

▶ *Make it fun.* You are, after all, asking these people to donate their time, so create a pleasant atmosphere.

▶ *Listen to every piece of advice.* Stop talking and listen. You don't have to follow every piece of advice, but you need to hear it.

▶ *Provide feedback to the board.* Good or bad, let the board know what you did and what the results were.

Basic Office Equipment

As tempting as it may be to fill up your office with an abundance of clever gadgets designed to make your working life easier and more fun, you're better off disciplining yourself to buy only what you need. Consider these basic items:

▶ *Typewriter.* You may think that most typewriters are in museums these days, but they actually remain quite useful to businesses that deal frequently with pre-printed and multipart forms, such as contracts and shipping documents. A good electric typewriter can be purchased for $100 to $150.

tip

Consider managing forms electronically. Many software packages, including PDF Expert (https://pdfexpert.com) and Adobe Acrobat DC (https://acrobat.adobe.com/us/en/acrobat.html), allow you to scan paper-based forms into a computer or tablet once, and then electronically fill out the forms, and then store/share completed forms. This allows you to create a more paper-free work environment, plus gives you quick access to forms from any internet-enabled computer or mobile device, especially when your documents and forms are stored in the cloud (online).

► *Computer(s), Software, and Printer(s).* You do not necessarily need the "latest and greatest" in computer power, but you need a system that can run the software you need for your business and is expandable to accommodate your growth. For software, you have an abundance of programs to choose from that will support every aspect of your business—and more are being introduced virtually every day. Because software can be a significant investment both in terms of dollars and time in learning, do a careful analysis of your needs and then study the market and examine a variety of products before making a final decision. Keep in mind, many online applications, including Microsoft Office 365 and the specialized applications for freight brokers that are offered by DAT Solutions, LLC., do not require software to be purchased. Instead, you pay a monthly, per-user fee to fully utilize the software application.

► *Internet Access.* High-speed and reliable internet access is essential for any efficient business operation, especially a freight brokerage. Your choices will typically include a cable service, FiOS (fiber optics), cellular, or satellite, although not all these options will be available in every area. The type of equipment you'll need depends on how you'll be accessing the internet, and prices can vary depending on the service you need. Shop around for the best service and price package.

► Something Old, Something New

Should you buy all new equipment or will used equipment suffice? That depends, of course, on which equipment you're thinking about.

For office furniture (desks, chairs, filing cabinets, bookshelves, etc.), you can get some great deals buying used items. Remember, few people are ever likely to see your office, so make your choices based on functionality rather than appearance. You might also be able to save a significant amount of money buying certain office equipment used, such as your copier, phone system, and/or fax machine. However, for technology-based items, such as your computer, you'll probably be better off buying new. Don't try to run your company on outdated technology.

To find good used equipment, you'll need to shop around. Check out used office furniture and equipment dealers. Also check the classified section of your local paper under "Items for Sale," as well as notices of bankrupt companies and companies that are going out of business.

▶ *Data and Equipment Protection.* You need an uninterruptible power supply to keep your computer from going down in the event of a power failure or brownout, as well as a surge protector to protect your system from power surges. You can buy these items separately or as a combined unit. You'll also need a data backup system that allows you to copy the information from your computer to another location for safe storage. Consider investing in some type of online backup (cloud-based) option for storing or backing up your data, so it's always accessible, from anywhere.

▶ *Photocopier.* The photocopier is a fixture of the modern office and is necessary for even the smallest freight brokerage. You can get a basic, low-end, no-frills personal copier for less than $200 in just about any office supply store. More elaborate models increase proportionately in price. If you anticipate a heavy volume, consider leasing.

aha!

Postage stamps come in a wide array of sizes, designs, and themes and can add elements of color, whimsy, and even thoughtfulness to mail. Stamps look more personal; metered mail looks more "corporate." Consider using metered mail for invoices, statements, and other "official" business, and stamps for thank-you notes and similar marketing correspondence that could use an extra personal touch.

▶ *Fax Machine.* With the ability to easily scan and email documents, the need to send and receive faxes is declining quickly, but you will still want fax capability in your freight brokerage. Your options include a stand-alone fax machine, a multifunction printer with fax capability, adding fax capability to your computer, or using an online fax service. By installing the appropriate app (such as JotNot Fax, Tiny Fax, eFax, or FaxFile), your tablet or smartphone can also serve as a scanner and fax machine. Make your decision based on your anticipated needs and style of operation.

▶ *Postage Scale.* Unless all your mail is identical, a postage scale is a valuable investment. An accurate scale takes the guesswork out of postage and will quickly pay for itself. It's a good idea to weigh every piece of mail to eliminate the risk of items being returned for insufficient postage or overpaying when you're unsure of the weight. Light mailers—one to 12 articles per day—will be adequately served by inexpensive mechanical postal scales, which typically range from $10 to $25. If you are averaging 12 to 24 items per day, consider a digital scale, which is somewhat more expensive—generally from $50 to $200—but significantly more accurate than a mechanical unit. If you send more than 24 items per day or use priority or expedited services frequently, invest in an electronic computing scale, which weighs the item and then calculates the rate via the carrier of your choice, making it easy for you to make comparisons. Programmable electronic scales range from $80 to $250.

▶ *Postage Meter*. Postage meters allow you to pay for postage in advance and print the exact amount on the mailing piece when it is used. Many postage meters can print in increments of one-tenth of a cent, which can add up to big savings for bulk mail users. Meters also provide a "big company" professional image, are more convenient than stamps, and can save you money in a number of ways. Postage meters are leased, not sold, with rates starting at about $15 per month. They require a license, which is available from your local post office. Only four manufacturers are licensed by the United States Postal Service to manufacture and lease postage meters; your local post office can provide you with contact information. An alternative to a postage meter that will allow you to avoid buying stamps and making regular trips to the post office is to print your postage yourself through an online account.

  Several options are available for generating postage directly from your computer. For example, there's Pitney Bowes (www.pitneybowes.com), Stamps.com (www.stamps.com), Endicia (www.endicia.com), and ShipStation (www.shipstation.com/features). In addition to paying for the actual postage you need, a low monthly fee applies to use these services, and in most cases, a special printer is needed in order to create the postage from your computer.

▶ *Paper Shredder*. A response to both a growing concern for privacy and the need to recycle and conserve space in landfills, shredders are becoming increasingly common in both homes and offices. They allow you to efficiently destroy incoming unsolicited direct mail, as well as sensitive internal documents, before they are discarded. Shredded paper can be compacted much more tightly than paper tossed in a wastebasket, which conserves landfill space. Light-duty shredders start at about $25, and heavier-capacity shredders run $100 to $500.

Telecommunications

The ability to communicate quickly with your customers, carriers, and suppliers is essential. Also, being able to reach your employees when they are out of the office is important.

Advancing technology gives you a wide range of telecommunications options. Most telephone companies have created departments dedicated to small and home-based businesses. Contact your local service provider and ask to speak with someone who can review your needs and help you put together a service and equipment package that will work for you.

tip

Listen to your customers and carriers. If they complain that you're hard to reach or aren't returning calls promptly, it's time to reevaluate your communications system. Lost calls mean lost revenue.

You'll need reliable voice communication that is answered 24/7 by a human or an electronic system. Even if most of your shippers are local, it's highly unlikely that all of their customers will be, too. You'll want to provide a toll-free number so nonlocal shippers, consignees, and trucking companies and their drivers, who don't have free or flat-rate long distance, can reach you without having to make a toll call. Most long-distance service providers offer toll-free numbers, and they have a wide range of service and price packages. Shop around to find the best deal for you.

Many small business office phone systems can forward calls to a smartphone, making it easier for someone to reach you during or after business hours, when you're not sitting at your desk. In fact, if you're the only employee at your freight brokerage business, there are mobile apps available for the iPhone and Android smartphones that provide the advanced features of a business phone system. For example, there's Sideline, iPlum, eVoice, WiCall Business, and Business Line, which are available from the App Store (iOS) or Google Play App Store (Android).

Keep Your Customers Out of Voice Mail Jail

Voice mail is one of the most popular modern business conveniences and can be an efficient communication tool. But keep in mind that the pace of the freight industry is so rapid that there isn't always time to return calls, so whenever possible, answer your phone yourself—and insist that your employees do likewise—and handle calls as quickly and smoothly as possible.

If you use an automated answering system, be sure to tell callers how to reach a live person. Ideally, that information should come very early in your announcement. For example, your greeting might sound something like this:

Thank you for calling ABC Freight Brokers. If you know the extension of the person you are calling, you may enter it now. To reach an operator, dial zero at any time during this message. For dispatch, press one. For tracing, press two. For billing, press three. For a company directory, press four.

Transportation Brokerage Software

Technology has made starting a freight brokerage easier than ever, and there are several software packages on the market designed specifically for brokers. See the Appendix for a partial list of resources. In addition, you can get off-the-shelf word processors, spreadsheets, accounting programs, and other software functions to help you run your business. Instead of purchasing the Microsoft Office suite of applications outright and then needing to upgrade the software each time a new version is released, Microsoft offers the Office 365 option. For a monthly fee (around $10.00 per user), you have full access to all Office applications (Word, Excel, PowerPoint, Outlook, OneNote, etc.), and all software updates are included.

"By spending money upfront on computer and communication technology, you are saving money in the long run," says Cherry Hill, New Jersey-based freight broker Bill Tucker. "You'll also have a lot more sales appeal with the ability to provide information to customers."

Website and Email

Websites are no longer optional for businesses, and your email address should include your company domain name, which should lead to your company's website. It's fine to use an email service such as AOL, Gmail, Hotmail, or Yahoo! for your personal email, but it detracts from your professional image when you use it for business.

Your website is one of the primary ways prospective customers will find you, and it's a key way for you to communicate with your existing customers. A well-designed, easy-to-navigate, optimized website is essential.

Study the websites of successful freight brokers, and make notes of the elements that appeal to you as well as the ones that don't. Then when you have a clear vision of what you want your website to look like and what you need it to accomplish take the project to a website designer.

Use Online Content to Educate Your Customers

One of the most efficient and effective ways to promote any business is through content marketing, defined by the Content Marketing Institute as "a marketing technique of creating and distributing relevant and valuable content to attract, acquire, and engage a clearly defined and understood target audience—with the objective of driving profitable customer action."

Some people refer to content marketing as education marketing. The idea is to provide information that has value to your audience through your online content. You can share and promote that content through a variety of ways, and one of the most popular is social marketing. But if you're going to do it, you need to do it right.

The two primary components of social marketing are media and networking. Social media are websites and applications used for social networking. Social networking is the use of dedicated websites and applications to communicate informally with other users or to find people with similar interests to oneself.

Perhaps the biggest challenge of social marketing is the number of platforms available and the rapidly changing popularity of those platforms, which is why we're not going to give you how-to lessons on specific social media sites. It's not necessary for you and your freight brokerage to be active on every social network. A smarter strategy is to pick the two or three networks that are most popular with your market and establish your presence on them and not worry about the others. Having a company Facebook page (separate from your personal Facebook page) and a presence on LinkedIn is advisable. And you don't need thousands of fans and followers; you need customers and prospects who are engaged with you online.

These steps will help you get started:

1. *Set clear goals for your social marketing efforts.* Be specific and keep those goals in mind with everything you do. If a particular initiative isn't likely to help you meet an objective, don't waste time doing it. Along with setting goals, determine how you're going to measure results.

2. *Dedicate the human resources to social marketing.* You need someone on your team (and it could be you) who understands social marketing, is comfortable with the platforms you'll be using, and has the time to manage your social marketing program. It's better to not do social marketing at all than it is to start it and let it fall by the wayside.

3. *Be prepared to produce sufficient content.* Content is the fuel for your social marketing vehicle, and without it, your efforts will stall. Content includes blogs, special reports on critical transportation issues, images, videos, infographics, comments, and so on. It's okay to share content from other sites (with appropriate permission and attribution, of course), but you should also be creating your own original content.

4. *Prepare your website for social media attention.* One of the desired results of your social media efforts is to increase traffic to your website. Make sure your marketing message across all of your online activities is cohesive and synergistic.

5. *Remember that it's a conversation.* Don't simply talk at your audience; engage with them. Ask for input. Create content that's so great they'll want to share. And don't let their questions or comments go unanswered.

6. *Be realistic in your expectations.* Don't anticipate monumental results for a minimal investment. Also, remember that not everyone on social media is your "friend"—these are customers (or prospects), and they may use your social platforms to complain. If they do, handle the issue as quickly and efficiently as possible, using the situation as an opportunity to demonstrate your superior customer service.

Your Social Media Policy

An important part of your overall management and marketing strategy is your social media policy. This is different from your on-the-job internet policy. You need guidelines for what employees can—and can't—say about the company whenever and wherever they are online. In the past, workers who had a bad day would go home and grumble about it to their families or to their buddies over drinks after work; today, they're far more likely to vent on the internet, and what they say could damage your company.

Points your social media policy should address include:

▶ *On which sites and under what circumstances employees can identify themselves as employees of your company.* Online business networking has value and should be encouraged, but if employees are involved in activities outside the workplace that may be considered divisive (such as hot political and social topics), you may not want to risk alienating customers by being publicly identified with those issues. Don't try to keep employees from expressing their opinions; just make it clear that they are not to connect the company to those opinions or actions.

▶ *Protecting confidential and proprietary information.* It may sound like a no-brainer, but your policy should specifically include a prohibition against revealing confidential information on social media sites.

▶ *Prohibit disparaging the company, its employees and suppliers, and its current, previous, or prospective customers.* Social media sites are a popular place for people to vent, but your employees need to know that if they've had a bad day and they're ticked off at the company, their boss, or a customer, they can't put it up on a social network in any way that would identify the company, the customer, or the individuals involved.

Have your policy reviewed by an attorney to make sure it doesn't violate employees' free speech rights or other applicable laws or regulations. Provide employees with a copy of your policy and have them acknowledge in writing that they have received and understand it. Finally, enforce the policy consistently without exception.

Inventory

Because the only thing you sell is service, you'll require very little in the way of inventory—but what you do need to keep on hand is important.

You'll need to be sure to maintain an adequate stock of marketing materials, including brochures, business cards, promotional/marketing items, etc. You'll also need to maintain an ample supply of administrative items, including checks, invoices, letterhead, paper, and miscellaneous office supplies (including printer ink or toner).

Company Vehicle

Though you won't be hauling freight yourself, you will do a substantial amount of interacting with your customers at their places of business, and you'll meet with truckers at their terminals and offices. You will also need to attend various professional and networking functions. You can either use your own vehicle or have your company purchase or lease a vehicle that you use for business.

Because you may have customers and/or colleagues riding with you, choose a four-door sedan that is roomy and comfortable. It should also have a sizable trunk so you have plenty of space to carry files and supplies (and a set of golf clubs, if you play).

Remember that your automobile is essentially your mobile office, and you will be judged by its appearance. Keep it clean, both inside and out. Wash it regularly to avoid a buildup of road grime, and do not allow trash and papers to accumulate inside. If you smoke, empty the ashtray daily and use a deodorizer for the comfort of your nonsmoking passengers. (Sure, it's your car, and if you want to smoke, that's your business, but remember that buying decisions are often based on emotional factors, then later justified with logic and reason. A nonsmoker who is offended by a smoker will find a way to avoid doing business with that person.)

Staffing Your Company

You can start and run a successful brokerage as a one-person business, but to really grow, you're eventually going to need employees. If you find the idea of interviewing, hiring, and managing employees somewhat intimidating, you're not alone— that's a common feeling among entrepreneurs. But this is very much a people business, and the people you hire will be critical to the success of your company, so it's in your best interest to do it carefully and wisely.

The first step is to define the job you plan to offer. Create a detailed job description that outlines what the person's responsibilities will be, as well as what skills, experience, education, and personality type you want them to have. The more detailed you are when defining and writing out each job description, the easier it will be for you to find a perfect applicant to fill each position.

When Cathy Davis started MCD Transportation in Smyrna, Tennessee, she was her company's only employee. Today, the business she has passed on to her daughters has five full-time people. When Cherry Hill, New Jersey-based freight broker Bill Tucker bought his late father's company, it was staffed by a few part-time, retired traffic managers. Today, there are some 30 people on the payroll, plus a few commissioned salespeople who work as independent contractors. "We pride ourselves on realizing that this is a people business," he said. "It's incumbent on us to be able to attract and hold the best people we can."

Ron Williamson started RJW Logistics with him and his wife working part time. Today, he employs nearly 50 people in his Bloomingdale, Illinois office, plus about 150 drivers—mostly owner-operators—for his trucking operations.

aha!

The ability to find and hire competent employees is a skill unto itself. Simply getting along with a perspective applicant and liking their personality are important, but you need to be able to evaluate their skill set, experience, reliability, honesty, work ethic, professional reputation, and education, for example, all of which help to determine if someone will be a good fit for your business.

Instead of taking a costly trial-and-error approach, consider working with an employment agency or having someone with extensive human resources or headhunting skills work with you during the hiring process.

This chapter discusses some of the hiring issues that are specific to freight brokerages. For more general information about developing your own skills as a human resources professional, consider reading specialized business books or taking classes on this topic that are designed for small business operators.

Pay scales in the transportation industry are very much affected by geography and market. For example, an experienced dispatcher in Chicago could easily earn double what the same position would pay in Parkersburg, West Virginia.

Do some informal networking in your community to determine what the going pay scales and commission ranges are before deciding how much you're going to pay. Whatever you decide to offer in the beginning, from the day someone is hired, tell employees what they must do to get a raise without having to ask for it; then follow up by increasing their pay rates when they've earned it and have met specific milestones.

It's a good idea to hire people before you desperately need them. Waiting until the last minute may drive you to make hiring mistakes, which can

tip

The U.S. Small Business Administration's website (www.sba.gov/managing-business/running-business/human-resources) offers a handful of free articles and resources related to managing human resources as a small business operator.

▶ Develop a Human Resources Strategy

After you clearly define the job position you're looking to fill, use the resources at your disposal to find qualified applicants. These resources include referrals, social media (including LinkedIn), career websites, industry associations, and freight brokerage training programs that are looking to place their graduates into jobs. Of course, a traditional "Help Wanted" ad in a major daily newspaper can work too, but these days, career websites offer far more powerful recruiting tools.

Before you set up the first interview with an applicant, lay some groundwork to make the hiring process as smooth as possible. Decide in advance what you need. You know you need help, but exactly what kind of help? Do you need a salesperson or administrative support? Do you need a broker (agent), or someone to handle billing? In the beginning, you'll be looking for people to do the tasks you can't or don't want to do. As you grow, you'll be looking for people who can help you expand your capabilities.

> ▶ *Write detailed job descriptions.* Take the time to put a list of responsibilities and required skills in writing. This forces you to think through what type of person will best meet your needs. It also helps you reduce the risk of hiring the wrong person and allows you to establish expectations for your new employee(s) right from the start.

> ▶ *Set basic personnel policies.* Don't think that because you're a small company you can just deal with personnel issues as they come up. You'll avoid a lot of problems down the road if you set policies at the outset.

tip

Some of the more popular online job-related websites where you can post and promote your job openings to seek out qualified candidates include: Indeed (www. indeed.com), Monster (www.monster.com), CareerBuilder (www. careerbuilder.com), ZipRecruiter (www. ziprecruiter.com), and Simply Hired (www. simplyhired.com).

cost you dearly, both in terms of cash and customer service.

When you first begin hiring people, you may want to consider bringing them on as part-timers until your business grows to the point that full-timers are required. One of the biggest keys to getting and keeping good people is flexibility, and you will find plenty of talented folks who, for whatever reason, don't want to work full time.

If you can accommodate them, you'll both benefit. As the workload grows and you need a full-time person doing that particular job, either change the status of your part-timer or, if that won't work, be creative. Consider hiring a second part-timer, setting up a job-sharing situation, or some other solution that will allow you to retain a valuable person and still get the work done.

Basic Positions

Because the service you offer is pretty straightforward, you don't need a wide range of job titles in your company. Here are the basic positions you'll need to fill as you grow:

- ▶ *Broker (agent).* A broker does the basic tasks that you do. This person needs to understand all the details involved in arranging a shipment and have good communication skills. A background in trucking is helpful. Unless you have a full-time bookkeeper or accountant, you or your brokers will have to bill shippers and pay carriers. You can either pay brokers a salary or a commission based on their sales.
- ▶ *Secretary/receptionist.* In most freight brokerages, this individual answers the telephone, routes calls,

tip

Salary.com (www.salary. com) is a fee-based online service that helps employers determine salaries for employees based on a wide range of criteria, including geographic location. This can be a valuable tool to help you set salaries and put together overall compensation packages for your employees.

takes messages (during business hours, instead of relying on impersonal voicemail), greets visitors (though they will be infrequent), and handles routine word processing and correspondence.

▶ *Customer service/Account representative*. This is an inside person who handles all customer service duties, including quoting rates, taking pickup orders, tracking shipments, assisting customers with claims, and dealing with any service issues that arise.

▶ *Bookkeeper*. This individual keeps your financial records and may also handle billing and payables. He or she will also work as a liaison with your accountant.

▶ *Sales representative*. A sales rep may work inside on the phone, outside face-to-face, or a combination of both. This person's job is to identify and secure new business and help maintain existing business.

Keep in mind that as a small business operator, you and your employees will often juggle multiple responsibilities. Another important position within a freight brokerage is the person who manages the company's website, blog (if applicable), and social media presence.

Calling All People

Picture the ideal candidate in your mind. Is this person unemployed and utilizing various career websites to find a job? It's possible, but you'll improve your chances for a successful hire if you are more creative in your search techniques than simply writing a help wanted ad for a newspaper or posting a job opening on one or more career websites.

Put the word out among your professional contacts that you're looking to hire, and utilize tools offered on professional social networking services like LinkedIn (www.linkedin.com). The TIA (www.tianet.org) also offers resources for its members that can help freight brokers find and hire qualified employees. Schools and organizations that offer freight broker training, such as Brooke Transportation Training Solutions (www.brooketraining.com), are always willing to share details about their recent graduates who are looking for employment within the industry.

Evaluating Applicants

When you actually begin the hiring process, don't be surprised if you're as nervous at the prospect of interviewing potential employees as they are about being interviewed. They may need a job, but for you, the future of your company is at stake.

tip

Before you hire your first employee, make sure you are prepared. Have all your paperwork ready, know what you need to do in the way of tax reporting, and understand all the liabilities and responsibilities that come with having employees.

It's a good idea to prepare your interview questions in advance. Develop open-ended questions that encourage the candidate to talk. In addition to knowing what they have done, you want to find out how they did it. Ask each candidate the same set of questions and take notes as they respond, so you can make an accurate assessment and comparison later. If candidates claim to have experience, use industry jargon to see how well they understand it. The freight business has a language of its own that most outsiders won't be able to speak unless they've had proper training and experience in the industry.

When the interview is over, let the candidate know what to expect. Is it going to take you several weeks to interview other candidates, check references, and make a decision? Will you want the top candidates to return for a second interview? Will you call the candidate, or should they call you? This is not only a good business practice; it's also common courtesy.

Always check former employers and personal references. Though many companies are very restrictive as to what information they'll verify, you may be surprised at what you can find out. At least confirm that the applicant told the truth about dates and positions held. Personal references are likely to give you some additional insight into the general character and personality of the candidate; this helps you decide if they'll fit into your operation.

Be sure your employees are legal. Under federal law, you must verify the identity and employment eligibility of employees; complete and retain the Employment Eligibility Verification Form (I-9) on file for at least three years, or one year after employment ends, whichever period of time is longer; and do not discriminate on the basis of national origin and citizenship status.

aha!

Instead of hiring full-time or part-time employees, you can hire freelancers, develop an internship program, and/or work with independent contractors (agents). Each of these options requires you to adopt a different hiring approach, has different financial ramifications for your business, and allows you to fill different types of positions with qualified candidates. For small, startup businesses, these options often make more financial sense than initially hiring full- or part-time employees.

Be sure to document every step of the interview and reference-checking process. Even very small companies are finding themselves targets of employment discrimination suits; good records are your best defense if it happens to you.

tip

Hire people as soon as you start to feel you need them. You may be able to start by yourself, but to really grow and generate substantial revenue and profits, you'll need a team.

Benefits

Many of the employees you want could be working for major freight carriers or large manufacturers and already enjoying "big company" benefits. You can't afford not to offer a strong benefit package. The brokers we spoke with provide paid vacation and holidays, health and life insurance, retirement plans, bonuses, profit-sharing, and flextime. Any other benefits and perks you offer to employees that make their employment experience more enjoyable or save them money will also be welcome.

As a smaller company, you have a degree of flexibility large companies don't always have. For many people, especially those with children at home or care for elderly parents, flexible working hours can be a tremendous benefit.

Give your employees subscriptions to industry trade magazines and newsletters, and encourage them to use and share the information they learn from those publications. The cost is nominal, and the result is that you'll increase their value to the company as well as their sense of self-esteem.

Williamson says that in addition to tangible benefits, you need to create a pleasant working environment. "This is a high-stress business, and we try to make the job fun," he says.

Keep People in Perspective

There is no business where the slogan "people are our most valuable asset" is more true than in transportation, and taking care of your people is certainly important. But it's also important to keep the relationship of the individual to the company in perspective.

"When you hire people, you can never let them think they are more important than the company," says Indianapolis-based freight broker Chuck Andrews.

When he started his company, he hired a few people who brought business with them; they had an inflated opinion of their value to the company and used that to attempt to manipulate Andrews. Don't give in to this brand of professional blackmail. Of course, it's possible that when you lose certain employees you may also lose some customers—but it's also possible that you won't, and it's highly unlikely that the loss of one person can destroy your business if you've built it properly. Andrews stated, "You have to let employees know they're important to you, but you can't let them think they have you over the rack and can come and go as they want."

The High Cost of Turnover

Employee turnover is an important issue in the transportation industry, especially in sales and customer service positions. Remember, this is a relationship business, and when you have employees who have built strong relationships with customers and carriers, you have employees who will be the constant target of recruiting efforts by other companies.

aha!

Find out what your employees want in the way of benefits and perks before you spend time and money developing a package. Do a brief survey; ask what they think of the ideas you have and ask for their ideas. If they want something you can't afford to do, don't reject it immediately; figure out what you can afford, and explain the situation to the employee.

Some of the costs of turnover are fairly easy to calculate; others are essentially priceless. When someone leaves, you have the hard costs of paying overtime to other employees to get that job done until a replacement is found, of recruiting (advertising, screening, interviewing, etc.), and of training. Those numbers are fairly easy to figure. Harder to calculate is the cost in customer relations and goodwill. You may even lose a few customers who opt to follow the departed employee to a different broker or carrier.

Bill Tucker says the key to keeping turnover down is to avoid seeing your relationship as an employer-employee one, but rather as partners. That certainly includes bonuses and profit-sharing programs, but it goes beyond pure financial incentives. Employees need to participate in the decision-making process; they need to be encouraged to contribute ideas and solutions.

People also need to be treated with fairness and compassion. It isn't realistic to expect people to leave their personal lives at home. When employees need you to be flexible about family issues—whether it's taking a few hours off to watch a child perform in a play or needing help dealing with an elderly parent requiring full-time nursing care—it's not only kind but wise for you to provide as much assistance as possible. Along with doing the humane thing, you'll be building a level of employee loyalty that can't be bought for any amount of salary.

Why Train?

Training is an area of managing people that you can't escape. Many of your employees come on board with at least a basic knowledge of the work they must do. But even the most experienced need to be trained in your particular operation and procedures.

The transportation industry has an abundance of training opportunities, from formal courses of study at colleges and universities to special conventions and workshops to monthly professional association meetings. It's a good idea to support a variety of training opportunities. For example, MCD Transportation provides both formal and on-the-job training and maintains a company library with current publications. Employees are encouraged to work on their professional certification, and the company pays for related studies. The company also pays for costs related to membership and participation in professional associations.

warning

Sometimes small companies lose good employees to larger firms that have better career opportunities. They may not be attracted as much by the money and benefits as they are by the room to grow and advance. Do the best you can to offer career growth to your people.

Training Techniques

Whether done in a formal classroom setting or on the job, effective training begins with a clear goal and a plan for reaching it. Training falls into one of three major categories:

▶ Credential Potential

Gain additional respect for yourself, your staff, and your company by encouraging your employees to earn the Certified Transportation Broker (CTB) designation. The CTB credential was developed by the TIA to increase industry professionalism and integrity through a rigorous program of study and examination. Candidates complete a home-study course designed around academic scholarship and practical experience and then sit for a four-hour proctored exam to earn their credentials. For more information on CTB certification, contact the TIA at (703) 299-5700 or www.tianet.org.

orientation, which includes explaining company policies and procedures; job skills, which focuses on how to do specific tasks; and ongoing development, which enhances the basic job skills and grooms employees for future challenges and opportunities. These tips will help you maximize your training efforts:

▶ *Find out how people learn best.* Delivering training is not a one-size-fits-all proposition. People absorb and process information differently, and your training method needs to be compatible with their individual preferences. Some people can read a manual, others prefer a verbal explanation, and still others need to see a demonstration. In a group-training situation, your best strategy is to use a combination of methods; when you're working one-on-one, tailor your delivery to fit the needs of the person you're training.

With some employees, figuring out how they learn best is a simple matter of asking them. Others may not be able to tell you because they don't understand it themselves; in those cases, experiment with various training styles and see what works best for the specific employee.

▶ *Use simulation and role playing to train, practice, and reinforce.* One of the most effective training techniques is simulation, which involves showing an employee how to do something and then allowing them to practice the technique in a safe, controlled environment. If the task includes interpersonal skills, let the employee role-play with a co-worker to practice what they should say and do in various situations.

▶ *Be a strong role model.* Don't expect more from your employees than you are willing to do. You're a good role model when you do things the way they should be done all the time. Don't take shortcuts you don't want your employees to take or behave in any way that you don't want them to behave. On the other hand, don't assume that simply doing things the right way is enough to teach others how to do things. Role modeling is not a substitute for training. It reinforces training. If you only role model but never train your employees, your employees aren't likely to get the message.

▶ *Look for training opportunities.* Once you get beyond basic orientation and job skills training, you need to constantly be on the lookout for opportunities to enhance the skill and performance levels of your people.

▶ *Make it real.* Whenever possible, use real-life situations to train—but avoid letting customers know they've become a training experience for employees.

▶ *Anticipate questions.* Don't assume that employees know what to ask. In a new situation, people often don't understand enough to formulate questions. Anticipate their questions and answer them in advance.

▶ *Ask for feedback.* Finally, encourage employees to let you know how you're doing as a trainer. Just as you evaluate their performance, convince them that it's OK to tell you the truth, ask them what they thought of the training and your techniques, and use that information to improve your own skills.

Noncompete Agreements

To protect yourself from an employee leaving you to start his or her own firm that directly competes with yours, you may want to ask everyone who comes to work for you to sign a noncompete agreement. Noncompete agreements typically consist of time, geography, and industry restrictions, and their enforceability varies by state.

Have the language of your non-compete agreement created by an attorney who is familiar with employment law before you ask anyone to sign it.

Keep in mind that even though your employees sign non-compete agreements, they may choose to violate them. Then you will have to make the decision whether or not to take the issue to court.

Ron Williamson sued one former employee, a salesperson who started his own company. "We won, but we lost," he says. "It cost me about $32,000, and we settled out of court through arbitration, and recovered about $12,000 of that. I had to go to my customers and ask them to testify against this person. Noncompetes are tough, and they take an incredible amount of time [to enforce]."

That may be, but his willingness to sue helped when another former employee left the company. He started to violate the terms of his agreement but backed off when he realized Williamson would take action.

Marketing

As you now know, just about everything must move, at least part of the way to its destination, by truck. With this in mind, it is safe to say that almost every company is a potential customer for you. But if you take that approach, you'll have a tough time coming up with an effective, not to mention affordable, marketing plan.

What's wrong with just going after anybody in the world who might ever have to ship something by truck for any reason? Because that market segment includes literally millions of companies and individuals, and it's impossible for any small business to communicate effectively with a market that size. Can you afford to send even one piece of direct mail to one million prospective customers? Of course not. But when you narrow that market down to, for example, 500 or 1,000 potential customers located in a particular area, conducting a successful direct-mail campaign is much more affordable and manageable. In today's business world, direct mail, however, is a more antiquated form of marketing that's been replaced by online-based tools, resources, and social networking services.

aha!

One of the most effective ways to build your customer list is word-of-mouth. Provide excellent service to your shippers and you will increase the likelihood that they'll spread the word about your business to other shippers.

Keep these questions in mind as you form your marketing plan:

- ► Who are your potential customers?
- ► How many of them are there?
- ► Where are they located?
- ► How do they currently transport freight?
- ► Can you offer them anything they are not getting now?
- ► How can you persuade them to do business with you?
- ► Exactly what services do you offer?
- ► How do you compare with your competitors?
- ► What kind of image do you want to project?

The goal of your marketing plan should be to convey your existence and the quality of your service to prospective customers, ideally using a multifaceted approach that involves use of the internet, as well as targeted email.

Market Research

Market research provides businesses with data that allows them to identify and reach particular market segments and to solve or avoid marketing problems. A thorough market survey forms the foundation of any successful business. It is impossible to develop marketing strategies or an effective product line without market research.

The goal of market research is to identify your market, find out where it is, and develop a strategy to communicate with prospective customers in a way that will convince them to use you.

Begin by focusing on two broad areas: the people and firms you work with directly, such as carriers and shippers, and the general business trends that affect the industry as a whole. With this information, you will be able to move on to more specific research that will help you determine your target market, where to locate your business, what services to offer, and your geographic scope of operations.

Choosing a Niche

There are many valid reasons for choosing a well-defined market niche. By targeting a specific market segment, you can tailor your service package and marketing efforts to meet that segment's needs. You'll also develop a reputation for expertise that attracts new customers. For small business operators, marketing to a niche audience is one of the most useful features of the internet, as well as social networking services, like Facebook, Twitter, and LinkedIn.

One of the best parts of being a freight broker is that you build long-term relationships with most of your customers. Motor carrier freight service is rarely a one-time purchase; once a customer comes on board with you, you will likely get plenty of repeat business. However, most shippers use multiple carriers and brokers, which means you must take the time to find out as much as you can about shippers's volumes and needs and provide consistent service so they are comfortable coming back to you, and you can increase your share of their business.

"We become an extension of our customers' management style and/or traffic program," said Smyrna, Tennessee-based freight broker Cathy Davis. "We have a much larger carrier base than they do and usually have better negotiation skills, especially if it's a small shipper. We do the calling for them, which frees them to work on other projects. We know how to qualify carriers and have access to more information [about them] than the shipper does."

You can design your niche based on geography (either location of shippers or destination of freight), types of cargo (agricultural, perishable, oversized, bulk commodities, etc.), size of loads, specific industries, or some other special shipping need. To choose a niche, first consider what types of shipments and/or shippers you enjoy working with. Then conduct market research to determine if there is a sufficient demand for the services you want to provide. If there is, move ahead with your marketing plan. If there isn't, consider how you might adjust your niche to one that generates adequate revenue.

Communicating with Your Customers

Once you've selected a niche, you'll need to consider how to let the shippers in that niche know about you. This is the essence of marketing. Don't be discouraged if your marketing efforts don't produce an immediate response. This is a relationship business, and it takes time to build your reputation and the rapport you need with shippers. Also, remember that your marketing efforts support your primary sales efforts but rarely generate a sale on their own. Even so, they deserve your attention.

All your promotional and advertising materials (including your website and social media presence) must clearly indicate your status as a broker, must be under the name by which you are registered, and may not directly or indirectly represent your operation as a carrier. With that legal caveat out of the way, be sure all these items are professional and letter-perfect. Consistency is important; your business card, envelopes, letterhead, labels, invoices, promotional items, email signatures, website, social media accounts, blog, etc., should all have the same logo, use the same typeface, and use the same color scheme.

Small but useful giveaway items—such as pens, mugs, scratch pads, and baseball caps—are very effective in supporting your marketing efforts. Customers aren't likely to choose a broker based on these items, but it's important to keep your name in front of them in a positive way. Be sure the promotional items clearly and consistently identify your company and tell how to contact you.

Both online and offline directory listings are important so shippers can find you. Check with your local phone company to find out its advertising deadline and directory distribution date, and, if possible, plan to launch your business in time to be included.

tip

Set up an interactive website where customers can request rate quotes, and customers and carriers can contact you for other information via forms or email. In addition, always make sure your phone number is prominently displayed on every page of your website and within the profiles of your social media accounts. You want prospective customers to be able to find and contact you as easily as possible. Don't make them look for your phone number or email address when they visit your website or company Facebook page, for example.

For most freight brokers, a print Yellow Pages display ad will not be worth the substantial investment that goes along with it; however, you might want to give your listing some distinction by having it set in bold type or including a line or two indicating your specialties or market niche. More importantly, make sure your website gets listed on all of the major search engines (Google, Yahoo!, Bing, etc.), and that your business gets listed with other online-based directory services, such as Yelp!, even though you're not targeting consumers as your customers.

Broadcast (radio and television) advertising is generally not effective for freight brokers, but some print advertising (within industry-specific publications that cater to your niche audience) will help build your credibility and name recognition. Look for publications that shippers in your target market read; if you're not sure what they are, ask some of the shippers you'd like to have as customers. Your ads do not have to be wildly creative; in fact, a better approach is to simply say what you do and why you do it well in an abbreviated format and then include your company name, your logo, and how to contact you. Keep the design of the ad clear and uncluttered; don't cram so much text into it that no one will read it. Some great places to begin your print advertising are in the newsletters of your local transportation organizations.

You will also want to create a brochure that describes what you do. A basic 8.5-by-11-inch, three-panel piece is sufficient. It should include your company name, address, phone, and fax numbers; website and email addresses and other contact information; your logo; a detailed list of the services you provide; a brief description of your background to establish credibility; and a benefits statement that tells shippers why they should use you.

Once the brochure is created in printed form, make sure you offer the same content as part of your website, Facebook page, and any other online presence that you manage. For example, the printed brochure can be offered online as a downloadable PDF file, or the same content can be displayed as part of an interactive webpage.

Use a professional graphic designer and copywriter to produce your ads, brochures, and website content. All printed materials should be professionally printed; don't just run them off on your laser printer or a photocopy

tip

A more targeted approach to paid advertising is to use online search engine advertising via a service like Google AdWords (https://adwords.google.com). These campaigns are inexpensive to create and launch, highly targeted, and can generate results very quickly. You can get started for a little as $50.

machine. Your prospective customers will be able to tell, and you'll look like an unstable, fly-by-night operation.

Know Thine Enemy

One of the most basic elements of effective marketing is differentiating yourself from the competition. One marketing consultant calls it "eliminating the competition," because if no one else does exactly what you do, then you essentially have no competition. However, before you can differentiate yourself, you first need to understand who your competitors are and why your customers might use them.

As a freight broker, you'll be competing with other brokers, freight forwarders, carriers, and probably some types of transportation consulting firms. To a degree, you'll also be competing with your customers' internal traffic departments.

Finding out about your competitors isn't difficult. In many cases, you'll know their people from your own industry networking, perhaps from previous jobs or professional associations. Your customers and potential customers will usually be very open about what they like and don't like about other service providers. The key is to pay attention, take notes, and use what you learn in your own marketing efforts.

Outsourcing Opportunity

As you plan your marketing strategy, consider how the trend of outsourcing can help your brokerage. Outsourcing is the practice of contracting with an outside firm to handle tasks that are not part of a company's core business. For example, as a freight broker, your core business is to link shippers and carriers, so you may choose to outsource such tasks as certain accounting procedures, some of your marketing functions, or perhaps the technical work involved in building a website and blog (and managing your company's social media accounts).

Many companies are outsourcing all or part of their shipping functions. Brokers are in an excellent position to offer themselves as an outsourcing resource, essentially functioning as the customer's traffic department. You can

aha!

Establish yourself as an expert by writing articles for transportation trade publications and blogs, as well as the trade publications and blogs your target market reads. If you don't have the writing skills and/or the time to compose articles yourself, hire a professional writer to ghostwrite (write under your name) them for you.

relieve your customers of all the work related to transportation and traffic management, save them money, and improve their service.

"A number of our smaller customers use us for their entire shipping and receiving business," says Bill Tucker. "Not only on the traffic management but also some of the purchasing and acquiring of products." This type of consulting service does not require any particular license—just knowledge and the ability to provide the service.

Of course, it's not a good idea to go to the traffic manager and pitch yourself as a supplier who wants to take over his job. You'll have a much better chance of succeeding if you approach a senior person in the organization whose interest is finance, such as the CFO.

"You may go in and try to eliminate the traffic manager's job," says Indianapolis-based Chuck Andrews. "[Try to] convince the vice president of finance or the president of the company that by using your service, he can do away with one person. If [you are talking about] a traffic manager who is wearing multiple hats, [your sales position is that] you are there to assist him and make his job easier."

Join the Right Groups

Professional associations offer a variety of networking and educational opportunities. If you're serious about being a freight broker, you'll want to join several organizations, some industry-exclusive and others more general.

Some of the associations you may consider include (see the Appendix for contact information):

▶ Transportation Intermediaries Association
▶ Delta Nu Alpha
▶ National Association of Small Trucking Companies
▶ National Association of Women Business Owners (for women-owned brokerage firms)
▶ Local transportation and traffic clubs
▶ Your local chamber of commerce
▶ A lead exchange or small local networking group

It's a good idea to belong to the local transportation clubs in all the cities in which you do business. For example, Andrews belongs to three transportation associations in Indianapolis where his company has its headquarters, plus clubs in Chicago, Cincinnati, and other major areas where he does business. He doesn't attend every single meeting, but he goes to the ones he can, and his name and company are listed on the membership rosters. "We get phone calls out of the blue from people who see our name on those rosters," he says.

Done correctly, marketing can really give your business a boost—especially in the beginning, when you need it most. Keep in mind, marketing and sales are two different tasks that require different skill sets. The goal of marketing is to find and attract interest among perspective customers and clients (in your case, shippers). The goal of sales is to take the leads generated by your company's marketing efforts and transform them into long-term paying customers.

Sales

The freight industry involves the buying and selling of an intangible service, which makes it a strong "relationship" business. Success as a freight broker requires that you do a tremendous amount of both face-to-face and telephone sales. In other words, your written and verbal communication skills need to be top-notch, and you need to have an outgoing and social personality.

Don't let the word "selling" scare you. Most of the world's top sales professionals will tell you they hate "selling." What they mean is, they hate the vision of the slick, fast-talking character on the used car lot or the door-to-door peddler who wedges a foot in the door and won't leave until you buy. But that's not "selling" in the professional sense of the word.

When you sell as a freight broker, you convince shippers that you have the capability to help them with their shipping needs better than anyone else—and if you don't believe that, then you need to be in another business. You are not going to browbeat them into using you, nor are you going to manipulate them into buying a service they don't need. You're going to provide the best professional service that meets their needs at a competitive rate, and communicating that is a major part of the sales process.

Your goal when it comes to sales is to identify the need of the customer for what you're offering, and then quickly, concisely, and in the friendliest way possible, clearly demonstrate how working with your freight brokerage can save the customer time, money, and aggravation. Focus on how what you're offering will directly benefit the prospective customer and solve one or more of their problems while filling one or more of their immediate and/or long-term needs. Pinpoint problems and offer proven and money-saving solutions.

Telephone, Online, or Face-to-Face Sales

You might hate the telemarketers who call your home at precisely the moment you are sitting down to dinner, but when it comes to selling your own service, a telephone call can be a very powerful tool.

RJW Logistics has a sales rep who generates $2 million a year in gross revenue just by calling people on the phone. The transportation industry used to be very much a "good old boy" system of casual, drop-in sales calls. It consisted primarily of telling a few jokes, leaving behind some promotional swag, and asking for a shipment by saying something like "Got anything going my way?"

Today's transportation professionals don't have time for unexpected visitors with no clear agenda. Collectively, they're spending billions of dollars each year to move materials, and they need those goods to arrive on time, in good condition, at a reasonable and competitive price.

This is not to say that you shouldn't be friendly and personable. In fact, your personality plays an important role in the growth of your business. But each sales contact should have a clear purpose that ultimately provides a benefit to your customer. Most customers appreciate a systematic, sophisticated approach that doesn't waste their time.

In today's intensely competitive environment, the majority of brokers mix telephone, online communication (emails), and face-to-face sales, using the phone to pre-qualify and set appointments, making a personal call, and then following up on the phone and by email. Once someone voluntarily provides you with their email address, this is often the ideal way to communicate with them after a business relationship has been established. Most people can access their email from their computer(s), smartphone, and/or tablet—at work, at home, and while on-the-go. A growing number of people prefer to communicate via email because it's more efficient.

Of course, when using email, be clear, concise, and professional within your messages. Focus on correct spelling and avoid punctuation mistakes. Use complete sentences and always stay on point. Use business language and avoid including emojis or internet shorthand, like TTYL (talk to you later), BRB (be right back), or LOL (laugh out loud), within your messages.

Qualifying Prospects

The first step of the sales process is qualifying the prospect, which is sales training jargon for determining how much business the potential customer has and who makes the decision as to who is going to get it.

This is not as hard as it seems. It really involves asking a few simple questions. If you networked your way into the company, you probably have a pretty good idea of the answers. If you're cold calling, simply ask the receptionist or operator "Can you give me the name and title of the person in charge of choosing carriers for your outbound shipments?"

It is important to ask for the name and the title before you ask to be connected with that individual. Of course, sometimes operators will transfer your call, but when they don't, you begin the conversation with the advantage of knowing whom you're talking to and the ability to call that person by name.

warning

Be careful that you don't patronize or insult the support staff of your customers or prospective customers. Keep in mind that these people may not only influence the decision-making process, they also may eventually be promoted to decision-making positions—either with that company or another one. So treat them with respect, be concerned about their needs, and nurture a professional relationship with them.

Once you're on the phone with that person, confirm that you are indeed talking to the decision-maker. The receptionist may have referred you to the shipping clerk, who fills out the freight bills, calls carriers, and handles some tracing functions—but who does not actually make the decisions. Don't be shy about asking this question. Most companies these days operate "lean and mean," and workers don't have time to listen to a sales presentation they don't have the authority to act on.

Remember, you need to identify the real decision maker (and keep in mind that there may be more than one in many companies), but don't ignore the decision influencers. As the name indicates, these are the people who are in a position to influence the decision-making process. They could be telephone operators, receptionists, administrative workers, shipping and receiving clerks—even high-ranking corporate officers.

tip

Instead of playing voicemail tag, you may find it beneficial to ask for a prospect's email address and then send that person a short, personalized, and well-written introductory email message. After an initial in-person sales meeting, you can use email to follow up.

Think about this: Say you and another broker are competing for a major piece of business from a particular company. The plant manager is making the decision, and his goal is to find someone who can work well with his shipping clerk so he can delegate the details and focus on other things.

You and the other broker are offering very similar rate and service packages, but the other broker took the time to talk with the shipping clerk, maybe even took him to lunch, and established a relationship you don't have. With all else being nearly equal, if the plant manager asks the shipping clerk for input in the decision, who do you think he's going to recommend?

This doesn't mean you need to wine and dine every shipping clerk at every company you deal with or that you need to send all the receptionists' flowers and candy every week. What it means is that you respect their roles in the process and you communicate with them to find out what they need and how you can best meet those needs.

Determining Needs

Once you've confirmed that a business has freight you can handle and you know who makes the routing decisions, you need to find out what they need before you begin telling them what you can do. It's a waste of their time and yours for you to do this any other way.

For example, why bother to spend time telling them about the wide variety of equipment you can provide, only to find out 20 minutes later that they only need standard trailers? Besides wasting time, that sends a clear message that you're far more interested in making the sale than you are in your customer. Before making a sales call, get to know as much about a prospect and their needs as possible. You can often learn a lot by visiting a prospect's website, for example.

So how do you find out what a prospective customer needs? Simple: Just ask or do some online research. Say something like "Before I tell you about our services, I'd like to ask you a few questions to find out exactly what you need. Can you tell me about your outbound freight?" Most of the time, you'll get more information than you need. Have a notebook handy and take notes while your customer talks; don't count on being able to accurately remember all the details of weights, commodities, and destinations. Most importantly, never say "no" to a customer. When they need something you can't provide, offer them an alternative instead.

tip

Before your first sales calls, do some research on the companies so you know how to approach them. Find out what they do, what they ship, and who the decision-makers are. Are they senior executives looking to improve service and save money or a traffic manager who will see you as a threat? "If you go in the wrong way, you're dead in the water," says Indianapolis-based freight broker Chuck Andrews.

Why Do You Ask?

When a customer (or a prospect) asks you a question about your capabilities, try to determine what's behind the question before you answer it. This lets you answer in the most positive and appropriate way possible.

Consider this scenario: You are in Charleston, South Carolina, making a presentation to the traffic manager at a midsize manufacturing firm. She asks "Do you work with any carriers that go to Des Moines, Iowa?" The short—and honest—answer is that you do not. So rather than lie, you simply say "No, I'm sorry." And you've lost every ounce of sales momentum you've built to that point.

But suppose you respond to her question with a question of your own. You might say "Why do you ask?" or "Do you have shipments going to Des Moines?" If she says the reason for her question is that she ships a truckload a week to Des Moines, you can ask more questions about the move and her needs and offer to get back to her after you've had a chance to find a carrier with a more competitive rate and service package than she has now.

But if she says "No, we don't ship out there, but one of our senior managers just left us to take a job with a company there, so I was just thinking about that city," you can avoid a flat "no" answer and instead emphasize your flexibility and willingness to shop until you find what your customers want.

This is a technique you can apply to just about any situation and relationship. Suppose your spouse says "Are you hungry?" If you just say "yes," you might find yourself presented with a gourmet home-cooked meal—or being dragged out the door to a restaurant you didn't really want to go to. It's always better to know what's behind the question before you answer.

Steak or Sizzle

If you've ever taken a basic sales course, you've probably heard "sell the sizzle, not the steak." What that means is you need to understand the difference between features and benefits—and focus on the benefits.

A feature is an aspect of the service you provide; the benefit is what the customer gains from that aspect. For example, the fact that you will call the shipper with delivery notification within two hours of the freight being unloaded is a feature. That the shipper has the peace of mind of knowing that the freight has been delivered on time and in good condition is a benefit. That you have access to thousands of carriers is a feature. That by using your firm, your customers are assured of getting the equipment they need when they need it is a benefit.

Before you ever call or visit a prospect for the first time, put together a presentation that includes needs identification and benefits selling, and practice it. Don't worry that you'll sound rehearsed; the reality is that the better you know your stuff, the more natural and confident you'll appear.

aha!

Turn maintaining current customer records into a sales opportunity for your business. Call every customer at least once a year, and say something like "We're checking our records for accuracy and completeness." Go through the information you have and then say, "Do you have any needs we haven't discussed that we might be able to help you with?"

Does Anyone Object?

Another long-time sales training phrase is "handling objections." That sounds much more frightening than it really is. In most professional sales situations, an "objection" comes in the form of a question, and whether it's a question or a statement, it is usually a request for more information.

For example, a prospective customer might say something like "How many carriers do you have agreements with?" or "I know you're new; I'm not sure you have the experience I need." Both of these statements might be seen as objections, but they really are chances for you to tell the prospect about the benefits he or she will gain by using you.

It's important to keep in mind that while freight may not appear particularly glamorous, for most companies the efficient and timely movement of cargo is critical to their ongoing operations. Selecting a broker or carrier is not a decision most shippers make lightly or casually. You'll find your customers very much involved in both the sales process and in the ongoing service. You've chosen a highly interactive business, and you can expect your customers to view you and your staff as the service.

Ask for the Business

One of the most difficult parts of a sales call for most people is the close—but it shouldn't be. If you've been paying attention—if you identified your prospect's needs and determined that you can satisfy them, if you've focused on benefits rather than features—then asking the prospect to make that final commitment should be a natural evolution of the sales call.

▶ Inward Bound

Beyond talking to the traffic manager or the shipping department, also build a relationship with the purchasing department. As part of the terms of their agreements, many buyers have the right to select the mode and carrier. In many companies, the traffic department gets involved in routing these shipments, but there are still plenty of businesses where purchasing and traffic work independently. If you can make a purchasing agent's life easier by helping him find the most economical and efficient method of moving inbound freight, you'll have a steady stream of business.

Here's one approach that works well: Find out what internal procedure the customer would have to change to give you his or her business. This is a simple matter of asking: "If you were to decide to let us handle your next load to Phoenix, what would you have to do?" When the prospect answers the question, perhaps with something like "I'd have to tell the shipping clerk to call you," ask if you can have the shipping clerk step in so you can answer any questions that person might have.

If the prospect resists, find out why. Say something like, "We've agreed that we have the services you need, that our rates are competitive, and we're in a position to provide some extras you're not getting now. Is there any reason why you shouldn't call the shipping clerk in now to give us a chance to prove ourselves on the next shipment?"

Prospects rarely say no without some sort of an explanation—an objection—that you'll have a chance to overcome. And even if you don't get the business—and you won't get it all—you'll at least know why.

Financial Management

One of the great things about the freight broker business is that it doesn't require a tremendous amount of startup cash to purchase facilities and equipment. Theoretically, you can get up and running with just a computer, fax machine, and telephone—but it does require a substantial amount of cash or a significant credit line, virtually from day one (unless you opt to be an agent for another brokerage).

Precisely how much money you need depends, of course, on your business volume, but you need to have sufficient cash on hand to pay your carriers on time, and that will likely be weeks before your shippers pay you.

This fact cannot be stressed enough: Cash-flow management is critical in this business. If you don't pay your carriers on time, they'll stop accepting your loads. Although the industry is huge, in many ways, it is also like a small town—everybody knows everybody else's business.

If you're not paying your bills on time, it won't be long before every carrier—and maybe even the shippers—find out about it. In a relationship business like freight brokering, a good reputation is essential, so protect yours by paying your bills on time.

You should monitor your cash flow constantly. Look at your receivables and payables on a daily basis. Cultivate fast-paying customers, and be sure your sales staff is explaining the need for prompt payment to new customers. There are specialized software packages designed for freight brokers that can help you properly manage your company's cash flow and finances. DAT Solutions, LLC (www.dat.com/solutions) is one company that offers a variety of software and online applications for freight brokers. What's great about these applications is that they're modular and expandable, so once you learn how to use the application, it can easily grow with your business.

Successful brokers tend to take a conservative approach to financial management. "We don't do a lot of borrowing," said Bill Tucker. "We have a great credit rating and good cash flow, but we don't want to just borrow and expand for expansion's sake. We're focused on service. We have a fiduciary relationship and responsibility to our carriers and to anybody else we owe money to, and to our employees."

Ideally, you'll open your doors with enough cash in the bank to pay all your expenses and your carriers until revenue from your customers (shippers) starts coming in. More practically, you may need to look at short-term credit options, such as unsecured commercial bank loans, borrowing against your accounts receivable, or selling your accounts receivable (a process known as "factoring," which is explained in more detail later in this chapter).

You may have a tough time with conventional loan sources, because by traditional lending standards, most freight brokers would not be considered bankable. Even if you have a record of paying your bills on time, you will likely need a revolving line of credit significantly higher than whatever assets you have to offer for collateral.

Setting Credit Policies

Because you are billing your shippers, or sometimes the consignees, you need to set credit policies and procedures. When you extend credit, you do so under the assumption that the customer intends to pay, is capable of paying, and that nothing will prevent him or her from paying. Most of your customers will be honest and dependable when paying their bills, but that doesn't mean you should blindly extend credit without first gathering and verifying information.

Each new customer should complete a credit application, and you should check the information he or she provides. This is standard practice in business. If a customer objects to completing a credit application, seriously consider whether extending credit to that customer is a safe thing to do. Look at it this way: When you extend credit for a service, you are essentially granting an unsecured, interest-free loan. Once the goods have been moved and delivered, you can't take back the service—and you (depending, of course, on the terms of your carrier agreement) are responsible for paying the carrier whether or not the shipper pays you.

Thanks in large part to the old Interstate Commerce Commission regulation that required payment of freight bills within seven days, most shippers have systems set up to pay freight bills faster than other invoices. "In the old days, it was regulation," Tucker said. "Today, it's entirely contractual among the parties. But carriers usually have pretty narrow margins. [Trucking companies have] a serious financial burden to carry. [They

▶ Tax Facts

You've probably heard this most of your life: The only two sure things in this world are death and taxes. Businesses—including freight brokers—are required to pay a wide range of taxes. Keep good records so you can offset your local, state, and federal income taxes with the expenses of operating your company. If you have employees, you'll be responsible for paying payroll taxes.

If you operate as a corporation, you'll have to pay payroll taxes for yourself; as a sole proprietor, you'll pay self-employment tax. Then there are property taxes, taxes on your equipment and inventory (minimal though it may be), fees and taxes to maintain your corporate status, your business license fee (which is really a tax), and other lesser-known taxes. Take the time to review all your tax liabilities with your accountant, and check out the taxes section in Entrepreneur Press' *Start Your Own Business* for more information.

have] to pay the driver, buy the fuel, buy the insurance, and make the loan payments on the equipment—all before the driver goes out the door."

Cooperative shippers understand the economic realities of trucking, and that if truckers are going to stay in business, they must be paid promptly. But you will still have customers who will take as long as you allow them to pay. It's your responsibility to set your terms and make those terms very clear to your customers.

You can include your terms (essentially when payment is due) on your credit application and have customers sign an acknowledgment that they know, understand, and agree to abide by your policies. On each invoice, clearly indicate the date the invoice will become past due.

Warning Signs

Just because a customer passed your first credit check with flying colors doesn't mean you should neglect to reevaluate their credit status. In fact, you should do it on a regular basis.

Tell customers when you initially grant their credit applications that you have a policy of periodically reviewing accounts so that when you do it, it's not a surprise. Things can change very quickly in the business world, and a company that is on sound financial footing this year may be quite wobbly next year.

An annual reevaluation of all customers on an open account is a good idea—but if you start to see trouble in the interim, don't wait to take action. Another time to reevaluate a customer's credit is when they request an increase in their credit line.

Some key trouble signs are a slowdown in payments, increased complaints, and difficulty getting answers to your payment inquiries. Even a sharp increase in volume could signal trouble; companies concerned that they may lose their credit privileges with you may try to milk you while they can, and if they aren't paying other brokers or carriers, they may have already lost some credit privileges and be looking to replace those sources. Pay attention to what your customers are doing; a major change in their customer base or product lines is something you may want to monitor.

Tucker says the process of providing good service to customers will also alert you to potential credit problems. "Just in the course of my relationship with the company, I talk to the president, I talk to the salespeople, I talk to the manufacturing people, I talk to the traffic manager, and even the guy who loads the trucks," he says.

Changes in a company's transportation needs and patterns can be early indicators of a problem. So what does Tucker do if he spots a red flag? "It depends on the details and on how serious it is. We may be [able to] help them solve their financial or market problem. But you also have to keep at arm's length if they are getting into trouble. You have to either quietly be 'running out of trucks,' or tell them the salesperson will be in there every Friday to pick up a check.

"It's our job to protect the money every way we can, including refusing to extend more credit and walking away from the business. Sometimes you just have to do that. But you have to know when, and you have to be able to evaluate those things. And we stay close enough to the customer so we can at least minimize the hit," says Tucker.

Most customers accept routine credit reviews as a sound business practice. A customer who objects may well have something to hide—and that's something you need to know.

Cash-Flow Controls

Certainly cash flow is important to any business, but it is critical to a freight brokerage. You need to keep sufficient cash on hand to pay your regular operating expenses and your carriers, but not so much that you miss out on revenue from alternative investments. In addition, you need to take steps to protect your company from internal theft.

Before you hire your first employee, set up internal controls to safeguard your assets and assure maximum cash flow management. One such control is to require proper authorization of transactions. Be specific as to which individuals are authorized to carry out what tasks, and hold them accountable for their actions.

You'll also want to establish a separation of duties so the person responsible for custody of an asset is not also responsible for record keeping that same asset. This prevents someone from stealing and then changing records to cover up what he or she has done.

Be sure the records you keep are adequate to satisfy financial and tax reporting requirements, as well as the

tip

Often, employees are motivated to steal by the feeling that they are being underpaid or that the business owner is making excessive profits on workers' efforts, so the employee feels "entitled" to steal. Help prevent this attitude by paying fair wages and treating your employees with respect.

federal regulations governing freight brokers. However, you should limit access to both assets and documents to prevent unauthorized use or theft; keep access on a needs-only basis.

Finally, set up a system to independently verify individual performance. Someone who was not involved in the work should check it for accuracy. This will help uncover intentional theft and fraud, as well as unintentional errors.

Beyond techniques to protect your assets, you'll also need systems to maximize them. Consider these:

► *Set up a sweep account.* This is a service banks offer that lets you earn the maximum interest on all the money in your accounts, even if it's just overnight, without penalties or concerns of bouncing checks. The system is set up so funds are automatically moved—or swept—in and out of the appropriate accounts each day. If your banker is reluctant to set you up with this type of an account, shop around for one who will.

► *Use a lockbox for receivables.* Another bank service, a lockbox, works like this: Your customers mail their payments to a post office box that your bank rents in your company's name. The bank sends a courier several times a day to clear out the box, checks are immediately deposited into your account—literally within hours of their arrival in the mail—and you get a report outlining all the transactions in as much detail as you want, as frequently as you want. Lockboxes mean you no longer have to run to the bank with deposits, or spend your (or one of your staff member's) valuable time opening envelopes, recording payments, and preparing deposits.

► *Accept electronic payments.* Talk to your banker about getting set up so you can accept payments through electronic transfers.

► *Invoice on a timely basis.* You can't expect customers to pay until you've issued an invoice, so get your invoices out as soon as you know what all the appropriate charges on a given shipment are. Be sure you include whatever documentation is necessary (copies of bills of lading, delivery receipts, etc.) for your customers to pay promptly.

warning

Mail thieves operate even in the nicest of neighborhoods, both residential and commercial. If you do not have a secure, locked mailbox and you receive checks by mail, rent a post office box so you know they'll be safe.

▶ *Enforce your payment terms.* Be prepared to follow up on late bills as soon as they become past due. Initial reminders don't have to be ugly or obnoxious, but you want to make it clear that you expect your customers to pay by the terms to which they agreed when they applied for credit.

The Power of Compensating Balances

One of the ways to measure the value of a company is its profitability. When it comes to the value of a company to a banker, the measure is in compensating balances. Though your ultimate net profit may be pennies on each revenue dollar, you are still funneling large sums of cash through your bank account as you collect from shippers and pay carriers.

Banks are very interested in companies with large amounts of cash flow. Even though the money doesn't really belong to you, you have temporary control over it. It will spend a certain amount of time in your account, and that time can be very important to a bank.

As you build your relationship with your banker, be sure to point out how much cash you expect to move through your accounts—it's called compensating balances—and ask what types of services and/or concessions the bank can provide you because of it.

Managing Payables

Due to the nature of the industry, paying carriers on time is critical. In fact, Bill Tucker says you are a financier of sorts for the carriers you use, because you'll likely be paying them before you get paid by your shippers.

While carriers make up the major portion of your payables, you have other bills to pay. Certainly on-time payment of all your bills is essential to building a good credit rating and maintaining a good reputation.

But by the same token, it is not good cash management to pay your bills before they are due. If your suppliers are willing to extend terms of net 30, then it's okay for you to

warning

As a broker, you'll collect and disperse a tremendous amount of cash. Resist the temptation to spend money that is already obligated to payables. "If they're not good money managers, that's where a lot of the startup brokerage operations get into trouble," says Indianapolis freight broker Chuck Andrews. "They see all this money and start spending it. Then it comes time to pay the bills, and there are no funds."

take 30 days to pay that bill—it's not necessary to pay it 10 or 15 days early. Keep your money working for you in your accounts for as long as possible.

Facts on Factoring

Factoring is the sale of accounts receivable to a third-party funding source for immediate cash. In a typical factoring arrangement, the client (you) makes a sale, delivers the product or service to the customer, and generates an invoice. The factor (the funding source) purchases the right to collect on that invoice by agreeing to pay the client the face value of the invoice

warning

According to freight broker Chuck Andrews, you need to watch your commission levels because if you are in a highly competitive area and working on margins that are less than the industry average, you may end up operating at a loss if you try to factor.

less a discount, typically 2 to 6 percent. The factor pays 75 to 80 percent of the face value immediately and forwards the remainder, less the discount, when the customer pays.

Because factors are not extending credit to their clients, but instead to their clients' customers, they are more concerned about the customers' ability to pay rather than the financial status of their clients. That means a company with creditworthy customers may be able to factor even though it couldn't qualify for a traditional loan.

Though the principles are the same, factors vary based on the type of businesses they handle, the amounts of invoices they purchase, and the specific services they provide. Choosing a factor is like choosing a bank—you have to find the right match.

Though factoring is almost as old as commerce itself, it was used primarily by very large corporations until the mid-1980s. Since then, awareness of factoring has grown, and more companies are incorporating this weapon into their cash management arsenal. Even so, there are still plenty of misconceptions about factoring.

Though factoring is often confused with accounts receivable financing, it's important to understand that this is not a loan, and it does not create a liability on your balance sheet. Rather, it is the sale of an asset, which in this case is an invoice for goods or services received by the customer.

Factoring is also considered one of the most expensive forms of financing, and while it may appear so at first glance, that's not necessarily true. The factor's fee is generally higher than the interest rate a traditional lender charges, but you need to also consider that factors provide a wide range of services that banks do not. They can help with credit checks, take over a significant portion of the accounting function for you, and generate reports to help you track your financial status.

Once you get a handle on money matters, you should be well on your way to running a successful freight brokerage.

Tales from the Trenches

By now, you should know how to get started and have a good idea of what to do—and not do—in your own freight brokerage. But nothing teaches as well as the voice of experience. This chapter features quotes from established freight brokers discussing what has contributed to their success and what they think causes companies to fail.

Use Advertising and Marketing Techniques that Work

Track your marketing efforts so you can concentrate on the techniques that work and eliminate the ones that don't.

Smyrna, Tennessee freight broker Cathy Davis said small giveaway items, such as pens, notepads, caps, and T-shirts, work well. Company newsletters (or a blog) with personal and industry information also get a good response. She said donations to fundraising events may be helpful (depending on the event and the degree to which it's promoted), but the impact of website sponsorships is questionable. She recommended developing a three-panel printed brochure that is easy to include with letters, invoices, and checks.

Chuck Andrews, an Indianapolis freight broker, builds name recognition by placing periodic ads in association newsletters, as well as in annual association and industry directories.

Prepare for the Future

It's understandable that at this point your primary focus is getting started, but you also need to think about the future. Develop a succession plan that is reviewed and revised annually. Know how leadership will be transferred when it becomes necessary—either through voluntary or involuntary departures.

Don't Reinvent the Wheel

Look around for good ideas and good products that people are already using that you can incorporate into your operation. Everything you do doesn't have to be original; get ideas from other brokers, carriers, shippers, and even totally unrelated businesses.

Bloomingdale, Illinois freight broker Ron Williamson learned this the hard way when he hired someone to develop a proprietary computer system. "That was a mistake because it was not a totally integrated system that would save us time and make us more efficient," he recalled. "Later on, we found a packaged program that had all the bells and whistles we needed."

Get Rid of Carriers That Don't Perform

Every trucking company will have an occasional service problem, but when the service failures become chronic, drop the carrier from your roster. "You won't keep your customers very long if you're having constant problems with your carriers," said Williamson. Of course, he acknowledged that in the beginning, you probably won't know who all the good and bad carriers are. While it's one thing to be understanding and give a carrier a second chance, you need to draw the line before the problems affect your own business.

Maintain a Broad and Diverse Customer Base

You need enough customers so that losing one—or even several—is not devastating. One of the biggest mistakes Cathy Davis ever made when she ran her freight brokerage was allowing one customer to control too much of her company's revenue. When that customer pulled away with very little notice, she was left scrambling to replace that business.

Get in the Spotlight

Because the freight industry is such a strongly relationship- and reputation-based business, it helps to put yourself in the public eye in a positive way as often as you can. Cathy Davis saw a favorable impact on her business from being the recipient of awards and by getting bylined articles published in trade publications. An even easier approach is to contribute content to online publications or well-trafficked blogs that cater to your industry or the shippers you are targeting as your perspective clients.

Be Open to Evolution

Though a freight brokerage is extremely lucrative on its own, it's also a business that can lead to the development of other transportation-related operations, from consulting to buying trucks and being a carrier. Cherry Hill, New Jersey, freight broker Bill Tucker, for example, offers a wide range of logistics services.

Andrews started as a broker, and then created his own separate trucking company to handle moves where the carriers he was using were short on equipment. Williamson also started as a broker and has since created two trucking operations.

Protect Your Reputation

"Focus on building the highest-quality reputation you possibly can," advised Tucker. "When a shortcut presents itself, but it's a little on the shady side, have the fortitude to pass it by, no matter how big the opportunity may seem. There are so many people in this industry who need good, solid, honest, reputable service—and long term, that's where the big money is. You survive, and you won't have a lot of doors closing to you because some bad story got out."

Tucker compares the industry to a small village. "Everybody knows everybody else's business. It's amazing how fast word travels. Nothing will put you out of business or limit your success faster than the story of one bad transaction or one nasty court loss because of bad practices getting out into the marketplace. You're going to have to sweat for a while, pull your belt in once in a while, and [endure] some tough times. But do it the right way every time, don't take any shortcuts, provide high-quality service, and maintain your integrity, and you'll always have customers willing to pay a fair price and good carriers that want to work with you."

An Industry Veteran Puts the Pieces Together

This book has provided a lot of information, originating from a wide range of credible sources, to help you develop a realistic understanding of what it takes to be successful operating a freight brokerage business.

Angela Eliacostas is the president and founder of Illinois' AGT Global Logistics (http://agt3pl.com), a successful freight broker that's been in existence since 2005. Eliacostas herself has worked in the transportation industry for more than 25 years. In this interview, she shares some valuable insight and advice to people first entering this industry.

Eliacostas literally grew up working in the transportation and trucking industry. "From the time I was born, my father worked in the trucking industry. From the time I was a young girl, I would go to work with him and help him in his business," she explained. "When I graduated from high school, I got married and had four children. I never went to college, but when I needed to go back to work, what I knew was the trucking industry. I wound up landing a job working part-time for a local trucking company."

As time went on, Eliacostas learned all aspects of the business she was working for and wound up being promoted to hold a wide range of job titles and responsibilities. When her boss retired, she was groomed to become the business and operations manager of the company she was working for.

In 2005, she decided to open her own freight brokerage business. "I was petrified to start my own business because I was a single mother raising four kids. I knew I was a survivor and a hard worker, and that no matter what happened, I would make operating my own business work," explained Eliacostas.

Over the years, AGT Global Logistics has experienced steady growth, despite the unsteady economy. "We have maintained the mentality of a small, hands-on freight brokerage business, which focuses extremely heavily on customer service. As the years have gone on, we have grown into a midsize company but have maintained our small company values, which I know our customers appreciate," said Eliacostas.

As of early 2017, AGT Global Logistics had 21 employees, and generated more than $10 million in annual revenues. "Years ago, freight brokerage companies had developed a very bad name in the transportation industry. They were considered untrustworthy, often fly-by-night operations. All a freight broker needed was a computer, a desk, and a phone, and they could operate from anywhere. If something went wrong, they'd close the business and reopen somewhere else under a different name.

"This has all changed, however. Over the years, the industry has evolved a lot, and the overall reputation of freight brokerage companies as a whole has improved. This is in part because of better regulation and the need for brokers to acquire higher value surety bonds, which help to ensure that everyone gets paid," said Eliacostas. "Today, all freight brokers are held to a much higher standard. These companies offer a specialized expertise that shippers in virtually all industries now rely heavily upon. It's important to understand that this is a relationship-based business in which offering the highest level of customer service is essential."

Eliacostas emphasizes that strong and long-term relationships must be established with carriers, who need to know that they will be paid on time. Similar and equally important relationships need to be created with shippers, who need to be able to trust your company. She explained, "By building up strong relationships with carriers, they are often willing to offer more competitive rates versus rates offered to a broker who doesn't have a close and long-term relationship. These lower rates get passed to our shippers, who rely on us to offer them the most competitive rates possible."

For someone looking to break into this industry, Eliacostas believes that the most important thing they can do is go out and work for a freight broker or logistics company and gain real-world experience. "Prior to launching AGT Global Logistics, I had worked in many different positions within the transportation industry, and I knew the industry very well. This experience proved to be extremely valuable. There is no job responsibility within my current business that I have not done personally," added Eliacostas. "It would be a huge disservice to enter into this industry without having a working knowledge of it. The best thing to do is to work for another company and take on different positions and responsibilities before setting up your own business."

Whenever Eliacostas goes about hiring a new employee for AGT Global Logistics, what she looks at most is someone's personality and how well they will fit into her organization. "I can train someone to do any job within my business. I consider my business to be a niche-oriented freight brokerage so having expertise about the industries we work with is essential. I bring applicants in for an interview, have them tell me about themselves, and then I look at their personality, and what I believe they can offer to my company," said Eliacostas.

Instead of focusing on education, Eliacostas looks at an applicant's past work experience. Her goal is to hire people who will fit into her established, dedicated, and loyal team. "We spend more time with each other than we do with our own families, so everyone working for AGT Global Logistics needs to fit in perfectly. I am very hands-on within my company. I have an open-door policy, and my employees see me working right alongside them. We are a united group working toward a single goal, which is to make the company successful," added Eliacostas.

Having good communication and follow-up skills is important, according to Eliacostas. She added, "As far as an applicant's education, I don't put a lot of emphasis on that. I don't require someone to be a college or tech school graduate. I look at someone's job history. What appeals to me is someone who has stayed with past employers for extended periods of time and who has demonstrated loyalty to past employers. Some of the most successful people I have ever met do not have a college degree. I believe education is important and have children who have pursued college, but most of my own education has come from life experience."

Over the years, Eliacostas has noticed more and more specialized freight broker training programs and certification programs being offered. She has mixed feelings about these programs. "People graduating from some of these programs are sometimes receiving incorrect or outdated training, which actually works against their chances of success. I have hired applicants who have completed freight broker training programs, but then wind up going around and around with them because they believe that everything they learned is correct, and what they already learned is by default the best way to do things within my company. These people have showed little flexibility to learn or adjust to how we do things, or to accept the more customized training that we provided. I have had my best luck hiring high school graduates who are willing to accept our training and pursue the training that we deem appropriate. These people are much more open to learning," said Eliacostas.

For people looking to gain real-world experience, Eliacostas recommends finding a job with a small to midsize freight brokerage business, as opposed to a larger company. This is because the smaller companies are less stringent and more open to exposing employees to a wider range of responsibilities. The pay might be lower, but the limitations put on employees are typically fewer.

Today's freight brokers need to be computer savvy. "We use computers for virtually everything we do. It's very important to be able to work the computer but also be able to communicate with carriers and shippers and maintain those personalized business relationships. AGT Global Logistics uses 3PL Systems, Inc.'s software [www.3plsystems. com], which is designed specifically for freight brokers," added Eliacostas.

Although there are many well-established small-, medium-, and large-size freight brokerage businesses already out there, Eliacostas believes there's always a way for new businesses to successfully enter the industry. "For someone coming into this as a newbie, find your niche. Find that specialized area where you believe you can make a difference. Be very defined in what you offer and the types of businesses you offer your services to. Do your research about the niche market, and then research each potential carrier and shipper you'll be working with," said Eliacostas. "Having a niche gives you a stronger focus and allows you to develop a specific area of expertise."

To find new clients (shippers), AGT Global Logistics continues to take a multi-faceted approach. The company relies on attending tradeshows, making cold calls, and scheduling in-person sales meetings with perspective clients. However, they also focus on using technology, including their website and social media, to pinpoint and generate new business.

She explained, "We believe in face-to-face communication. I believe in being persistent, without being obnoxious. Sometimes, it's a matter of being in the right place at the right time when it comes to landing a new client. It's not uncommon for us to touch base with a prospect every month, for two years or longer, before they give us any business. Persistence is essential."

Finally, Eliacostas believes that building a positive reputation for honesty is important. "When we're handling someone's business and something goes wrong, the shipper knows that we might not have good news, but we'll always provide the truth. They also know that we'll have a plan in place to fix or address the problem, and handle things correctly.

Our clients know we're always out in front of every situation, not hiding behind it. Our shippers know us and trust us, and much of that is because we maintain face-to-face, one-on-one contact with them. Plus, we have done our research and understand their needs and concerns," she concluded.

Freight Broker Resources

The following is a wealth of resources that will help you establish, manage, and grow your freight brokerage business, learn more about the industry, and achieve long-term success as a broker.

These resources are intended to get you started on your research. They are by no means the only resources out there. In addition to using the resources provided here, get out there and do some investigating in the real world and online.

Associations and Regulatory Agencies

American Trucking Associations
(703) 838-1700

950 N. Glebe Road, #210, Arlington, VA 22203-4181

www.trucking.org

Delta Nu Alpha

An international transportation organization with a focus on education.

(414) 764-3063

www.deltanualpha.org

Federal Motor Carrier Safety Administration
United States Department of Transportation

(800) 832-5660

1200 New Jersey Avenue SE, Washington, DC 20590

www.fmcsa.dot.gov

National Association of Small Trucking Companies

(800) 264-8580, (615) 451-4555, fax: (615) 451-0041

104 Stuart Drive, Hendersonville, TN 37075

www.nastc.com

National Association of Women Business Owners

601 Pennsylvania Avenue, NW, South Building, Suite 900, Washington, DC 20004

(800) 556-2926

www.nawbo.org

National Industrial Transportation League

7918 Jones Branch Drive, Suite 300, McLean, VA 22102

(703) 524-5011, fax: (703) 524-5017

www.nitl.org

Surface Transportation Board (STB)

395 E. Street, SW, Washington, DC 20423

(202) 245-0245

www.stb.dot.gov

Transportation Intermediaries Association

An organization for North American transportation intermediaries, including property
(freight) brokers, domestic freight forwarders, consolidators, ocean and air forwarders,
intermodal marketing companies, perishable commodity brokers, logistics management
firms, and motor carriers.

(703) 299-5700, fax: (703) 836-0123

1625 Prince Street, Suite 200, Alexandria, VA 22314

www.tianet.org

Truckload Carriers Association

(703) 838-1950, fax: (703) 836-6610

555 E. Braddock Road, Alexandria, VA 22314

www.truckload.org

U.S. Department of Transportation

1200 New Jersey Avenue, SE, Washington, DC 20590

(202) 366-4000

www.transportation.gov

Online Services and Resources

CoreLogic, Inc.

Credit reports, driver screening, and training.

(800) 872-3748

10277 Scripps Ranch Rd., San Diego, CA 92131

www.compunetcredit.com

FreightBrokersUSA.com

Online freight matching, broker software, and other resources.

www.freightbrokersusa.com

Getloaded.com

Online freight-matching service and other broker resources.

One Park West Circle, #300, Midlothian, VA 23114

(800) 474-8064, fax: (804) 744-8394

www.getloaded.com

Internet Truckstop

Online freight matching service, credit reports, and more.

(800) 203-2540

www.truckstop.com

DAT Solutions, LLC.
(800) 551-8847
8405 SW Nimbus Avenue
Beaverton, OR 97008
www.dat.com/products/broker-tms

Red Book Credit Services
(800) 252-1925, (913) 438-0606, fax: (913) 438-0690
10901 W. 84th Terrace, Suite 300, Lenexa, KS 66214
www.rbcs.com

Publications and Training Resources

Logistics Weekly and Logistics Journal
Offered by Transportation Intermediaries Association
(703) 299-5700, fax: (703) 836-0123
1625 Prince Street, #200, Alexandria, VA 22314
email: info@tianet.org
www.tianet.org

Leonard's Guide Online
Publishers of print and online directories for the freight transportation and warehousing
    industries.
(800) 574-5250
181 N. Vermont Avenue, Glendora, CA 91741
www.leonardsguide.com

New Broker Manual
Offered by Transportation Intermediaries Association. Includes training materials,
    sample contracts and forms, and FMCSA registration information.
(703) 299-5700, fax: (703) 836-0123
1625 Prince Street, #200, Alexandria, VA 22314
email: info@tianet.org
www.tianet.org

ThomasNet.com
Supplier, discovery, and product sourcing directories.

(212) 629-2100

5 Penn Plaza, New York, NY 10001

www.thomasnet.com

Transport Topics

Published by American Trucking Association.

www.ttnews.com

Software

DAT Solutions, LLC.

(800) 551-8847

8405 SW Nimbus Avenue

Beaverton, OR 97008

www.dat.com/products/broker-tms

Wolf Byte Software, Inc.

(888) 965-3298

5805 Whittle Road, #208, Mississauga, ON L4Z 2J1 CAN

www.wolfbytesoftware.com

Successful Freight Brokers

MCD Transportation, Inc.

Donna J. Wood, CTB, President

Dionne R. Kegley, CTB, Vice President

(615) 459-5343, fax: (615) 459-3353

P.O. Box 1197, Smyrna, TN 37167

email: operations@mcdtrans.com

www.mcdtrans.com

RJW Transport, Inc.

Ronald Williamson, CTB

(630) 424-2400, fax: (630) 424-7251

11240 Katherine's Crossing, Suite 400, Woodridge, IL 60517

www.rjwgroup.com

Tucker Company Worldwide, Inc.

William J. Tucker

(800) 229-7780, (856) 317-9600, fax: (856) 317-9699

56 North Haddon Avenue, Haddonfield, NJ 08033

www.tuckerco.com

Glossary

The following is an alphabetical listing of common terminology used by freight brokers and agents. The best way to develop a true understanding of these terms is to obtain some type of specialized training as a freight broker or agent, and/or land a job that will provide you with real-world experience working within the industry.

Accessorial charges: charges assessed by a carrier for services provided in addition to basic transportation, such as extra pickups, loading, and unloading.

Air-ride: trailers built to reduce road shock and designed to carry fragile items; the suspension system supports the load on air-filled rubber bags rather than steel springs.

Backhaul: the return trip of a vehicle from the destination back to the origin.

Bill of lading: a document that serves as the contract of carriage between the shipper and the carrier.

Bobtail: a tractor operating without a trailer.

Bracing: securing items inside a vehicle to prevent damage.

Break-bulk: the separation of a load into smaller shipments for delivery to ultimate consignees.

Claim: a charge made against a carrier for loss, damage, or overcharge.

Class rate: a rate constructed from a classification and a uniform distance system.

Commercial zone: the area surrounding a city or town to which rates quoted for that city or town also apply.

Common carrier: any person or agency publicly engaged in the business of transporting passengers or freight; common carriers are subject to two stringent obligations: compulsory service and liability for loss or damage to goods.

Consignee: the receiver of a freight shipment, usually the buyer.

Consignor: the sender of a freight shipment, usually the seller.

Consolidation: the collection of smaller shipments to form a larger quantity to get lower transportation rates.

Container (shipping container): standard-sized rectangular box used to transport freight by ship, rail, or motor carrier.

Contract carrier: a company that transports freight under contract with one shipper or a limited number of shippers.

Cost per hundredweight (cwt): an amount charged per hundred pounds of freight.

Density: a physical characteristic of a commodity, which is important in rate-making since density affects vehicle utilization; determining density requires measuring its mass per unit per volume, or pounds per foot.

Detention: the charge assessed by the carrier when the shipper or receiver holds a truck or trailer beyond the time allowed for loading and unloading.

Doubles (twins, twin trailers): a tractor and two semitrailers that are connected.

Drayage: a motor carrier that operates locally, providing pickup and delivery service.

Driver assist: when a driver is asked to assist in the loading or unloading process; sometimes treated as an extra charge on a per-hour or flat rate.

Driver's log sheets: a log of miles traveled, hours of driving, off-times, and rest periods that drivers are required to keep.

Dry van: a nonrefrigerated, noninsulated semitrailer handling general commodity freight that can withstand outside temperatures without suffering damage.

Empty backhaul: when a truck returns empty from the destination to the point of origin and therefore does not generate return-trip revenue.

Exclusive use: a request made by shippers that means their freight is the only freight on the truck.

Exempt carrier: a for-hire carrier that is exempt from economic regulations.

Expediting: determining where a shipment is during transit and attempting to speed up its delivery; many big companies have expeditors on staff who do this full time.

Flats (or flatbeds): a flat, solidly built trailer designed to handle heavier and bulkier loads than a dry van, such as metal, equipment, and machinery.

FOB: a term of sale that defines who is to pay transportation charges for a shipment, who is to control the movement of the shipment, or where title to the goods passes from the seller to the buyer; originally an acronym for "free on board."

For-hire carrier: a company that provides truck transportation of cargo belonging to others and is paid for doing so.

Freight bill: the carrier's invoice for transportation charges for a particular shipment.

Freight broker: the middle person who connects shippers and carriers.

Freight payable: technically, a freight bill that needs to be paid; in common use, it also refers to the special payables department large shippers may have that is dedicated to paying freight bills.

Freight pool: a collection of trailer loads waiting for assignment to a driver and tractor.

Front haul: the initial movement of the vehicle from the origin to the destination.

Full truckload (FTL): a shipment occupying the entire trailer, typically with a weight of 30,000 pounds or more.

Gross weight: the total weight of the goods being shipped, including packing and packaging materials.

Hazmat: Hazardous materials, as classified by the U.S. Environmental Protection Agency (EPA); transportation of hazardous materials is strictly regulated by the U.S. Department of Transportation.

Incentive rate: a rate designed to encourage shippers to ship heavier volumes per shipment.

Interline: two or more motor carriers working together to haul a shipment.

Intermodal: combining two or more modes of transportation, such as truck and rail, truck and air, or rail and ocean.

Interstate Commerce Commission (ICC): a federal regulatory agency that was abolished in 1995.

Joint rate: a rate over a route that involves two or more carriers transporting the shipment.

Just-in-time (JIT) inventory management: an inventory management technique designed to reduce inventory levels by delivering parts just as they are needed on the production line.

Layover: a delay preventing a driver from unloading as scheduled at destination; some carriers charge an additional fee for this.

Less-than-truckload (LTL): a shipment occupying less than the entire trailer, typically with a weight of less than 30,000 pounds; it can be combined with other shipments to make up a full truckload.

Less-than-truckload (LTL) carrier: a trucking company that consolidates less-than-truckload cargo for multiple destinations on one vehicle.

Motor carrier (MC): a company that provides truck transportation.

Multiple drops: a delivery requiring more than one stop.

Net weight: the weight of the goods being shipped, excluding the packaging and packing materials.

OS&D: an acronym for "over, short, and damaged."

Over (overage): when the piece count of a shipment is more than what is indicated on the bill of lading.

Over-the-road: a motor carrier operation that reflects long-distance, intercity moves; the opposite of local operations.

Owner-operator: a trucker who owns and operates his own truck(s).

P&D: pickup and delivery.

Pallet: a movable platform, usually made of wood, for the storage or transportation of goods.

Pallet exchange: the process of replacing a shipper's pallets, leaving an equitable number of empty pallets when picking up goods loaded on pallets, then picking up a comparable number of empty pallets from the consignee when the freight is delivered.

Payload: the weight of the cargo being hauled.

Peddle run: a truck route with frequent delivery stops.

Private carrier: a carrier that provides transportation service of its own cargo to the firm that owns or leases the vehicles and does not charge a fee.

Process agent: a representative upon whom court papers may be served in any proceeding brought against a motor carrier, broker, or freight forwarder; freight brokers are required to list with the FMCSA the names of process agents in each state where they have an office and write contracts.

Product (pro), load and invoice numbers: numbers assigned to shipments for identification purposes.

Pup trailer: short semitrailer, usually between 26 and 32 feet long, with a single axle; often used as doubles or triples.

Purchase order number: a number that buyers assign to their purchase orders that shippers will usually include on their freight documents so consignees can easily identify the load when it is delivered.

Ragtop: a box-like trailer open at the top, on which a large canvas is spread to protect cargo from the elements; primarily used for large, bulky bales or boxes, loose materials, and sometimes for nursery stock shipments.

Reasonable rate: a rate high enough to cover the carrier's costs but not so high that it enables the carrier to realize monopolistic profits.

Reefer: a refrigerated, insulated semitrailer.

Round trip: when a driver moves a load to a specific point, reloads at the point, and returns to the original point of pickup.

Semitrailer: a truck trailer supported at the rear by its own wheels and at the front by a fifth wheel mounted to a tractor or dolly.

Shipper order number: a number assigned to a load or shipment by the shipper for tracking purposes; this number should be referred to on invoices and any other documents concerning the shipment.

Shipping container: see container.

Shipping weight: the gross weight of a shipment, including product, packaging, and packing materials.

Short (shortage): when the piece count of a shipment is less than indicated on the bill of lading.

Short-haul discrimination: charging more for a shorter haul than a longer haul over the same route, in the same direction, and for the same commodity; this is an accepted industry practice since certain fixed costs apply no matter how long the trip is.

Skid: a pallet.

Split pickup: a pickup requiring more than one stop.

Tanker: a trailer shaped like a huge tank designed to handle liquid and loose, fine bulk materials.

Tariff: a publication that contains a carrier's rates, accessorial charges, and rules.

Tend to load: when the drivers attend to the loading and unloading of their trailers.

Truckload (TL) carrier: a trucking company which dedicates trailers to a single shipper's cargo, as opposed to an LTL (less than truckload) carrier which transports the consolidated cargo of several shippers and makes multiple deliveries.

Trailer on flatcar (TOFC): a method of moving cargo that involves transporting semitrailers on railroad flatcars.

Ton-mile taxes: taxes based on the weight (tonnage) of the shipment and the number of miles it travels (tax per ton, per mile).

Tracing: determining where a shipment is during the course of the move.

Tractor: a truck designed primarily to pull a semitrailer by means of a fifth wheel mounted over the rear axle(s); sometimes called a truck tractor or highway tractor to differentiate it from a farm tractor.

Tractor trailer: a tractor and semitrailer combination.

Traffic management: the management of the various activities associated with buying and controlling transportation services for a shipper or consignee or both.

Transit time: the total time that elapses from pickup to delivery of a shipment.

Trip leasing: leasing a company's vehicle to another transportation provider for a single trip.

Truckload (TL): the quantity of freight required to fill a trailer, usually over 30,000 pounds.

Weight per case: the total, or gross, weight per case, carton, or box.

Index